SPEED SECRETS

T0317954

THE LOST ART OF
HIGH-PERFORMANCE
DRIVING

How to Get the Most Out of Your Modern Performance Car

ROSS BENTLEY

Quarto.com

© 2017 Quarto Publishing Group USA Inc.
Text © 2017 Ross Bentley

First published in 2017 by Motorbooks, an imprint of The Quarto Group,
100 Cummings Center, Suite 265D, Beverly, MA 01915 USA.
T (978) 282-9590 F (978) 283-2742

Motorbooks titles are also available at discount for retail, wholesale, promotional, and bulk purchase.
For details, contact the Special Sales Manager by email at specialsales@quarto.com or by mail at
The Quarto Group, Attn: Special Sales Manager, 100 Cummings Center, Suite 265D, Beverly, MA 01915
USA.

ISBN: 978-0-7603-5237-3

Library of Congress Control Number: 2017934349

Acquiring Editor: Zack Miller
Project Manager: Madeleine Vasaly
Art Director: James Kegley
Cover Designer: Jeremy Kramer
Illustrations: Jeremy Kramer
Layout: Kim Winscher

Printed in USA

CONTENTS

ACKNOWLEDGMENTS

Mark Twain said, "There is no such thing as a new idea." And André Gide said, "Everything that needs to be said has already been said."

These quotes are true—mostly. When you dig down at the root of anything "new," it's often just a different spin on something that already exists, a combination of older thoughts and ideas or of existing concepts that have been elaborated in a new way. Truly unique ideas are rare.

What I write is the result of being able to think deeply about a sport that I'm passionate about: high-performance driving. I take what I've learned through experience and from others, and put it into a form that others can use in their own high-performance driving.

I am grateful to you, the reader, as I am to all of the drivers I've coached, trained, observed, or learned from. Every time I write something, I learn; the best way to really understand something is to teach it to others. Without an audience for my books, I wouldn't get to learn through the process of writing. Thank you for being part of my audience.

I would also like to sincerely thank the instructors and coaches I've worked with and around for nearly four decades, as well as the authors of books, articles, and videos I've absorbed in that time.

One of my most-used phrases is, "There's always more." Not long ago I thought, that's it, I'll never write another driving book again. I wasn't sure where I'd find enough new information to make it worth another book. But here I am again. Because, like driving, there's always more to learn, and I continue to learn.

Thank you to Motorbooks for helping me share what I love with you and others. Without a strong nudge from Zack Miller, this book wouldn't exist: he helped me see how this book could help driving enthusiasts.

In 2006, automotive journalist Mark Hacking contacted me and asked if I'd coach him for a day. He was writing a story about different learning methods for high-performance drivers. So we spent a day at Buttonwillow Raceway, where I introduced him to the mental and physical training approaches I use. We became friends and have stayed in touch through the years. As I dug into writing this book, I knew that I needed someone with a deep knowledge of the leading edge in automotive technology, both to check the accuracy of what I've written and to suggest additions. Mark was that guy. He's easily one of the most knowledgeable automotive journalists in the world, and an accomplished driver, too: he races cars and tests some of the latest production cars all over the world.

Without Mark's contributions, this book would not be as good as it is. Thanks, Mark.

Speaking of automotive journalists who know their stuff, I want to thank Kim Wolfkill for writing the foreword. As editor-in-chief of the one magazine I've consistently read every month for the past 50 years, *Road & Track*, it's an honor to have someone with his knowledge and experience about cars—and his exceptional driving ability—share his thoughts here

Finally, as always, thanks go to my wife, Robin, for helping me do what I love to do.

FOREWORD

KIM WOLFKILL
EDITOR-IN-CHIEF, *ROAD & TRACK* MAGAZINE

Walk into most any new-car dealer and it's hard not to marvel at the impressive machinery on display just waiting to be driven. From sleek GT coupes and luxury sedans to sports cars and SUVs, the array of choices is as diverse as it is enticing. Never before has such a high level of performance, technology, and engineering expertise been available to purchase right off the showroom floor. Needless to say, modern high-performance vehicles are faster and easier to operate than ever before.

As editor-in-chief of *Road & Track* magazine, I have the good fortune of driving the latest new cars and meeting the development teams that create them. To a person, these designers and engineers are passionate about building the best vehicles they can. They integrate as much advanced technology as possible with the ultimate goal of making products that are safe, capable, and enjoyable to drive.

This ongoing technological evolution has led to developments that go well beyond once-groundbreaking tech like anti-lock brake systems and traction/stability control. Those features are now standard on nearly every vehicle and, in many cases, are supplemented by newer advances like active accident avoidance, selectable performance modes, and even semiautonomous driving capabilities. All of this new tech is generally a good thing, especially when it helps make the roads a safer place to drive. But does it also make us better drivers? And, perhaps most importantly to enthusiasts, are we still having fun?

In addition to driving and testing lots of cars, I also have the good fortune to call Ross Bentley a friend. We've known each other for years, and before that

I admired his skills behind the wheel of many a race car. Ross is one of the best drivers, coaches, and people I know, so I can't think of a better person to help enthusiasts maximize their cars' most important performance feature: the driver.

While best known for his Speed Secrets series of racing-focused instructional books, Ross is not just about helping racers improve lap times or drive faster— he's about making everyone who climbs into a car a better driver. *The Lost Art of High-Performance Driving* does just that, tapping into his decades of professional coaching and instructing experience to clearly define and illuminate the meaning of "high-performance." Not so much from the car, but more so from the driver's perspective, he makes sense of the amazing tech that enables modern vehicles to be so capable. He identifies where technology is a welcome asset and where sound driving fundamentals are far more valuable than any electronic aid.

Ross combines clear explanations of vehicle dynamics with real-world instruction to make high-performance driving techniques easy to understand and easy to practice—and not only at a racetrack. Nearly everything learned in these pages can be honed on the street, on a favorite back road, or even on the way to work.

At the same time, this book isn't solely about becoming a better, faster, or safer driver; it's also about driving enjoyment. And as a lifelong automotive enthusiast, I think that may be the single greatest contribution Ross makes to car lovers everywhere. He teaches you how to do what you love even better. To get the most out of yourself and your car for maximum driving pleasure. Sure, you're a better driver for it, but you're also having much more fun. And for that, we all thank you, Ross.

– Kim Wolfkill

INTRODUCTION

WHAT IS HIGH-PERFORMANCE DRIVING?

There's no entry for high-performance driving in *Webster's Dictionary* or in Wikipedia, so we can't turn to any "official" definition for help.

Instead, here's how I describe high-performance driving: *doing, or performing, everything behind the wheel at the highest level possible*. It's maximizing your performance in all areas of driving, from parking to cornering on a racetrack, from smoothly progressing in rush-hour traffic to matching revs to make a smooth downshift. Yes, to be a high-performance driver, you don't even need to drive on a racetrack.

I have a story that illustrates what I mean. In the late 1980s, a friend and I started a high-performance driving school (yes, I've been at this for a very long time!). As anyone who's started a small business knows, it's a lot of work: I worked seven days a week, usually for at least twelve hours. I wasn't getting a lot of sleep. In fact, I often found myself driving home around 11:00 p.m. after conducting an all-day course at the track. I was yawning, trying to keep my eyes open.

At first, I stayed awake with the adrenaline from the thrill of teaching students to drive still rushing through my veins. Eventually, though, I needed something else; it's not that the thrill had gone away, I was just used to it.

A couple of miles from home one night, I drove over a particularly bumpy manhole cover, one that I knew was there and had usually avoided. For a moment, I had lost my focus. I knew I should have moved over in my lane to avoid the bump. Up to that point, my drive from the office had been near perfect. I had looked far ahead, driven with two hands on the steering wheel, and used the wheel and pedals smoothly. I'd read the traffic around me to decide which was the best lane to drive in, driven in nice arcs through corners so I could smoothly accelerate out of them, felt every little movement of the car, and had complete control over it. Also, I hadn't driven beyond the speed limit. Until I hit that manhole cover, it had been almost flawless.

That's when I made executing the perfect drive my goal each and every time I got behind the wheel of a car, no matter where I was driving. Trying for that perfect drive helped me become—and essentially identified me as—a high-performance driver. I was striving to perform all aspects of driving at the highest level. This kept me focused and awake.

To this day, I've never achieved the perfect drive. But I keep working at it.

What makes a drive perfect may be different for you, but I think there are many things we'd agree represent driving "perfection." These are the focus of this book. I'll revisit this at the end of the book.

With a clearer definition of high performance comes a question: why do we care?

You probably wouldn't have picked up this book if you didn't already have an answer. But there are a few specific reasons you might want to be a high-performance driver:

- The sense of satisfaction in controlling a vehicle, knowing that you've done something that many people can't (or aren't even concerned with)
- The pure thrill that comes from sensing and using a vehicle's limits (and its speed)
- The feeling of being in the moment and present in the act of driving
- The simple enjoyment that comes from working with the controls to make the car do what you want it to do
- The satisfaction that comes from continually learning more about and improving your driving

IS HIGH-PERFORMANCE DRIVING A LOST ART?

Current automotive design uses devices and technology that isolate and remove the driver from the act of driving. Some say that the art (and, I'll add, science) of high-performance driving is dying. What will be the point, once autonomous vehicles that we no longer even own transport us from point A to point B? It'll be a world of driverless vehicles.

There are still people who enjoy the art and science of driving, though. They understand and appreciate the difference between mere transportation and driving, especially high-performance driving.

Bob Lutz, former CEO of Chrysler, is one of the "giants" of the automotive industry. In the March/April 2016 issue of *Road & Track*, he said:

The automobile will remain a gigantic industry, now as a sports instrument or as a vehicle for enjoyment. Consider the horse. With the advent of the car, horses were essentially banned from streets. But they made a very nice comeback on private property. Dude ranches, farms, riding stables, racing. I think the same thing can happen to the automobile. Independent driving will become the equivalent of going to an upmarket horse event on a weekend.

I love that: "a vehicle for enjoyment."

That's what high-performance driving is all about: enjoyment. And until we're all being whisked around in autonomous vehicles, there's absolutely no reason why we can't enjoy high-performance driving on the road and

the track. Sure, as Lutz suggests, there may be a time when the track is the only place for high-performance driving, but until then—hey, let's enjoy this. And be as good as we can be.

This book is written from the perspective of driving on the street first, and on a racetrack second (if at all). That's not to say that we won't cover track driving, but how do you typically get to a racetrack? By driving on the road. So I'll discuss both driving on the road and on the racetrack.

HIGH-PERFORMANCE DRIVING: STREET VERSUS TRACK

I want to make one thing clear. When I talk about high-performance driving on the street, it doesn't mean driving fast. And it doesn't mean breaking the law in any way. This is not just some legal disclaimer type of thing so I don't get sued: I mean it. There's no need to drive illegally on the street to enjoy high-performance driving, or to be a high-performance driver.

You can never get enough track driving practice. But you probably spend most of your driving time on streets, so take advantage of that time. As I said, you don't need to drive fast to practice performance driving techniques. Part of being a high-performance driver is knowing when and where it's safe and appropriate to drive fast—on the track. You can still practice techniques when street driving that you can use to become a better track driver, and you can do that without driving fast. Build your "muscle memory" by driving the right way on the street. Be smart, and program your performance driving techniques.

Of course, the reverse is also true: driving on a racetrack can also make you a better driver on the street.

By my definition of high-performance driving, the actual goal is to drive as close as possible to the posted speed limit. It's part of the challenge, part of the enjoyment of striving to drive perfectly.

DEVICES, TECHNOLOGY, AND MORE

Let's shift gears for a moment (no pun intended). The list of driver aids, safety devices, and technology that equip vehicles today is mind boggling. I want to help you understand how some of these work, what they can and can't do, and how they benefit you.

While driver aids abound in modern performance cars, they each have limits to what they can do. Until we ride around in autonomous vehicles, the driver will continue to be the most important safety device.

I'm also going to cover some parts of driving, such as manual shifting, that some people consider old-fashioned and unnecessary.

Does a computer programmer need to know the history of computer science? Does a musician need to understand how a recording engineer mixes tracks? Does a tennis player need to know how to hit a backhand with one hand if he or she hits a two-handed backhand? The answer is no.

However, to be the best at what each of these people do, the answer would be yes.

Do you want the pilot of the plane you're flying on to know all aspects of flying, or just the bare minimum of what it takes to fly that exact plane? I don't know about you, but I'd rather my pilot knew how to manually fly a plane, even if the one I'm in is equipped with all sorts of technology to help them.

My point is that to be the very best high-performance driver you can be, you may need to learn some things that you don't use every time you drive. Maybe you drive a car with a paddle shift semiautomatic transmission, but you can still learn how to drive a fully manual, H-pattern transmission as part of developing as a high-performance driver.

SPEED SECRET

Program the "right" techniques on the street. Practice.

An interesting thing happens when you *do* understand things that may seem "old technology": you get better at driving what you have. You improve your ability to drive with the latest technology. Why? Because you understand the *why* behind what you and your car are doing.

You might feel that some of the discussion about technology and devices in this book is unnecessary, but I urge you to pay attention to these sections. Better yet, find an opportunity to actually practice using what is covered there: it'll make you a better driver.

Having said that, I won't get bogged down in the "old ways." In fact, I want to help you focus on new technology and how you can use it in a high-performance manner.

You may have no intention of ever driving on a racetrack, or maybe you're a "track junkie." What I write about in this book will help you become an even better driver. In other words, this book is for anyone who wants to improve and to be a high-performance driver—a driver who performs at a high level—regardless of your background and experience.

You know as well as I do that you don't learn to drive a car by reading a book; you learn by doing, by being behind the wheel and actually practicing. But I also know that a book like this can help you learn more in less time behind the wheel. It'll prepare you to make the most of every second you spend driving, and it'll help put what you experience when driving in perspective. It'll help things "click."

THE COMPETITIVE DRIVE

As I mentioned above, you don't need to race to be a high-performance driver. Where I draw the line between performance and race driving is the competition aspect. Performance driving is not about beating another driver—there are no "results," no trophies, no winners or losers. Actually, in performance driving, everyone's a winner.

Okay, before I get too philosophical here, I want to be clear that the winner in this "competition" is anyone who has fun learning to be an even better performance driver. There's often some competition in performance driving, but it's internal. It's the competition with oneself to improve, to beat your personal best. And I'd be a fool if I didn't think there weren't some comparing of lap times amongst friends at the racetrack. But that's not the purpose or intent of high-performance driving—it's secondary.

If you want to compete wheel to wheel, door handle to door handle, then I strongly recommend you go racing. This book can provide some basics for that sport. After all, the first step in racing is driving fast, and—well, that's part of this book's goal.

Whether you only drive on the street and highway, or whether you also head to a racetrack every now and then, this book is for you.

DRIVING TO THE LIMIT—YOURS

I'm going to make a big assumption and clarify something at the same time. The assumption? You want to drive your car at or near the limits of its performance. If it's capable of a "10" performance (with 10 out of 10 being the limit), you want to be able to drive it at somewhere in the 6 to 9.5 range (driving below a 6 could hardly be considered high-performance driving).

I understand that some drivers don't want to drive right at the very edge, since something might go wrong at that speed. There's nothing wrong with feeling that way, and everything I write about in this book still applies, even if you don't feel comfortable "pushing it to the limit."

If you want to drive at an 8 out of 10, then my goal is to help you drive there consistently. What you don't want to do is drive at 8 out of 10, then $^{10}/_{10}$, $^{6}/_{10}$, $^{11}/_{10}$ (oops), and so on. That's not driving consistently at the limit you've set, $^{8}/_{10}$.

If you want to drive at $^{10}/_{10}$, be prepared to accept the risk that comes with driving at that level, and do it in an appropriate place—a racetrack. Then I'll help you get there.

In my world, whatever limit you set is okay. A $^{10}/_{10}$ driver is not a better person than someone who drives at $^{8}/_{10}$. Of course, if you drive around a track at something less that $^{5}/_{10}$, you're really not high-performance driving.

When I talk about driving at the limit, I'm talking about the limit that you've set for yourself.

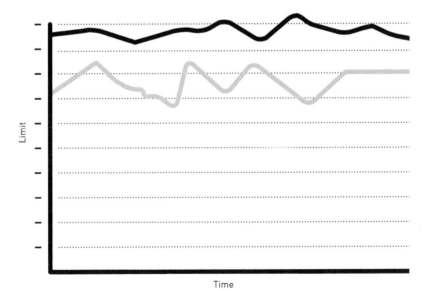

Time

No driver can drive right at the limit—at $^{10}/_{10}$—at all times, and most drivers choose not to for safety reasons. Understand your own limitations and the limits you're willing to drive.

GOALS FOR THIS BOOK

My goals for this book are:

- To help you be aware of your habits, good and bad, and build the best ones
- To prepare you to learn even more about driving every time you get behind the wheel of a car
- To provide you with the theory of high-performance driving, but also practical knowledge that you can use
- To help you understand your modern (or not-so-modern) car
- To further inspire you to constantly want to learn and improve your driving
- To have fun

HABITS: GOOD AND BAD

To expand on the first point I made above: a theme throughout this book, and one I rely on constantly, is this—you do what you do because you're mentally programmed to do so; in other words, you have habits. Also, you sometimes don't do what you want because you either don't have the mental programming to do it, or, every now and then, you access the wrong program (that is, you make a mistake).

Some habits—some mental programs—are good, and some aren't. Driving with two hands on the steering wheel is a good habit, while holding the wheel with one hand at the 12 o'clock position is not. Smoothly releasing the brake pedal is a good habit; snapping or popping your foot off the brakes is not.

A goal, then, is to break bad habits and build good ones. To succeed, you first need to be aware of which ones are good, which ones are bad, and how to change them. When you boil down everything I cover here, you'll see that this is the main purpose of this book.

HOW TO USE THIS BOOK

My advice to you is to read this book from front to back (although I won't be checking!), and then jump around to review certain sections when you need them.

Chapter 1 sets the stage with a discussion around the mindset of a high-performance driver. Then, Chapters 3 through 10 cover driving technique and knowledge as it applies to the type of car you're driving (with or without driver aids) and where you're driving (in traffic to work, on a twisty mountain highway, or on a racetrack).

Chapter 11 is aimed at driving on the street or highway, while Chapter 12 covers driving on a track. Chapter 13 is about the mental game of driving; Chapter 14 offers a final summary of what we've learned.

You'll also find short, quick summary tips, which I call Speed Secrets, throughout the book. They're meant to stick in your mind so you can recall key skills, techniques, and mindsets that will help you become the best high-performance driver possible.

Regardless of the speed at which automotive technology is advancing, I think this book will stand on its own for many years to come—because the focus is on technology in general terms, not on any one system, and on the details of how to be a high-performance driver. The focus here is on you, the driver (not on the car) and how you can use technology to be an even better driver than you are now.

There's one thing a high-performance driver is: *adaptable*. As technology changes, you will have the right mindset to adapt to it. That doesn't mean that past techniques will necessarily go away or be forgotten. In fact, understanding why an older technique was used—and perhaps continues to be used—is what's most important.

These are the two guiding principles that I urge you to keep in mind throughout your driving "career":

- There's always more—you can always learn more and improve.
- Have fun!

One of the best things you can do to improve your driving is work with a high-performance driving instructor in a safe facility—a racetrack.

1 THE PERFORMANCE DRIVER'S MINDSET

If had to pick just one thing that I've noticed through my near-four-decades of helping drivers improve that separates the best from the rest, it wouldn't be any one specific technique or skill. No, it's this: a burning desire to learn and improve, plus an open mind to new techniques and approaches.

It's that mindset that I know you have to some extent (you wouldn't be reading this if you thought you knew everything), and that I encourage you to build on.

Being a high-performance driver is all about performing at a high level. I suggest that being a high-performance *learner* is no different—and that's part of what makes you a high-performance driver.

As I said earlier, high-performance driving takes place both on the street and on the track. With that comes responsibility—you need to know when it's appropriate to push the limits of your vehicle, and when you should hold back.

RESPONSIBILITY

How many times have you spoken to a person who "brags" that he's been in a number of "accidents" that weren't his fault? I've talked to dozens of people who have made this claim. It makes you think, doesn't it?

Perhaps it's time these drivers took more responsibility for their driving actions, instead of feeling completely blameless when found "not at fault."

Many crashes in which a driver is found not at fault could be avoided altogether. In the past, I've witnessed two incidents that emphasize this.

Once, I was driving in the left lane of a four-lane road, next to another car. As we approached an intersection, the traffic light turned yellow. I began to slow to a stop, but the car beside me kept going. I noticed another car at the cross street waiting for the light to turn green. When it did, and ours turned red, the car proceeded into the intersection. The car traveling beside me ran right through the red light and T-boned the other vehicle. Fortunately, neither driver was injured—they were just upset and shocked.

The driver of the car crossing with the green light was "not at fault," and that's fair. But I could have told you many seconds earlier what was going to happen.

If only the driver had taken half a second to look before entering the intersection, the crash would never have taken place.

Another time, I watched as a dog ran out in front of a car I was following. The driver's only response was to slam on the brakes, and he steered straight into the dog. After stopping, the driver's comment was, "It's not my fault—the dog ran right out in front of me!"

Technically, he was right: it wasn't his fault. The road we were traveling on was quite wide, though, with large paved shoulders. Any driver should have been able to avoid the dog by slowing down and steering around it. Instead, his vision locked onto the object he wanted to avoid, while he slammed on the brakes.

As we'll discuss later, it's almost impossible to look at something and not hit it. The key in this situation would have been for the driver to recognize all the room to drive around the dog and to simply look and steer around the dog.

As drivers, we have a responsibility to try to avoid *any* incident on the road, even if it's not our fault. Too many people drive thinking only about themselves and their own actions (if they're thinking at all). All they're concerned about is who's at fault or who's to blame. As the above examples show, there is much we can do to respond to—and help correct for—others' actions (even those of wayward dogs). Who's "at fault" doesn't mean much when someone has been injured or killed.

As part of this sense of responsibility, you need to know where it's appropriate to drive fast, and where it isn't. The obvious place to drive fast is on a racetrack—something I highly recommend doing!

BE A ROLE MODEL

Being a high-performance driver is about being a role model for others. Set an example by driving smoothly and in control, and by behaving appropriately at all times.

You probably don't need much to be convinced that most drivers on the road today are less-than-ideal; they're not paying attention, they don't seem to care about being a good driver, and they're a challenge to drive around and near. No argument, right? So, why not put "the yawn effect" to use?

As you know, yawning is almost contagious. Good driving is the same. If you drive well, others around you will follow your example. Does that seem too idealistic?

SPEED SECRET

High-performance drivers take full responsibility for their actions, whether "at fault" or not.

Test my hypothesis. For the next month, go out of your way to set a good example for others:

- Pay extra attention to your driving and to the way others around you drive.
- Ensure you have a good-sized "bubble" around you, which means giving enough room between you and the car you're following.
- Control your speed, and don't get caught up in the "everyone else is speeding so I should too" syndrome.
- Don't try to enforce your speed on others by blocking lanes (especially the passing lane; make a pass, then move back to the right.
- Be courteous, or, as I prefer to look at it, be "collaborative."

If you look at driving on the street as a collaborative team effort, I suspect you'll change some of your driving behaviors.

As a car enthusiast or high-performance driver, you may be branded with a bad reputation: "You're crazy, drive too fast, and have your priorities all wrong. Why else would you spend all that money on your high-performance cars?"

Over the years, I've found that many car enthusiasts are some of the safest drivers on the road. Why? Because they care about driving. They care about their cars. They enjoy driving *and* they think about their driving all the time.

To these drivers, driving is a privilege to be enjoyed.

As driving enthusiasts, what can we do to improve the overall level of driving on today's roads? The best way is to lead by example.

You can spread collaborative driving with "the yawn effect." When you're deliberately and demonstratively collaborative, others will follow your example. If you let someone go ahead of you, that driver is more likely to be courteous to someone else, and so on. From your own experience you know that when drivers cooperate, traffic flows better—and everyone benefits.

Of course, there'll always be some drivers who take advantage of others and don't return the favor; that just seems to be human nature. But that really is the exception to the rule. Work with the odds, be collaborative and courteous, and notice how beneficial it is to you and others around you.

If you're a high-performance driver, people should hardly notice you on the street. You are subtle in traffic. You never make abrupt lane changes, never drive too fast, never take big risks, and you always drive smoothly. In fact, no one should even know you're on the road.

But if nobody notices you, how do you set an example? Start with your passengers. They may not even know what you're doing at first, but they'll figure it out eventually.

You should also set that example for your kids when they're in the car: they learn more than you might realize by watching you—and they'll be better drivers when they grow up. We learn more in the first five years of life than in any time after. How? Not by being taught, but by imitation: by watching what others are doing, memorizing or programming our brains (just like a computer), and then copying the behavior we've observed. We learn much through osmosis.

To have an effect on other drivers, drive with subtlety. Even when you're subtle, other drivers will be aware of your actions in, well, a subtle way. They'll be more likely to imitate your behavior and your actions, and they should become better drivers because of the example you set.

Drive calmly and in a relaxed manner, and others around you will also drive calmly. Drive at or near the speed limit, and others will follow your pace. Drive smoothly and with subtlety, and others will do the same. Drive collaboratively, and others will be collaborative as well.

If even 1 percent of drivers worked at setting a good example for others, it would make a positive impact on how everyone else drives.

Try it for yourself: for the next month, really concentrate on driving better and setting an example for other drivers to follow.

WATCH YOUR SPEED

Relax on your daily commute, stick to the speed limit, and not try to beat the other drivers around you to where you're going—I bet the time it takes to reach your destination doesn't change much at all.

But a number of things *will* change. Your fuel consumption will improve (and your vehicle will pollute the atmosphere less). You'll improve your chances of avoiding crashes (and, if you ever *are* involved in a crash, the damage will be less serious). You'll be far more calm and relaxed when you arrive. In addition, many other drivers around you will naturally follow your example.

It seems to be human nature. How often have you gone to pass a car on the freeway, and noticed the driver speed up to follow your pace? The same thing happens the other way around. If someone is passing you and you stick to your speed, that car will often slow down slightly to move in line with your pace.

If you are collaborative with other drivers, they'll return the favor to you— and to others as well. It's contagious. Try it. The next time there's a lane full of cars trying to merge with yours, wave the car next to you to go in front. Most times, that driver will do the same for someone else in the near future.

All this collaboration will help speed the flow of traffic. With the amount of traffic we have in cities and towns these days, that's really what it takes for you to get where you want to go in a reasonable amount of time. It's not how fast *you* drive but how well the traffic flows.

Now, I'm not naive enough to think that everyone is going to drive this way. Not at first, anyway. That's why I hope that just 1 percent of drivers will give it a

SPEED SECRET

Set an example and drive collaboratively. Others will follow, to everyone's benefit.

try. If that happens, it will naturally begin to spread. Even if a small percentage of drivers thought this way, over a period of time we would all notice a difference.

At one time I was involved with a program that promoted safer driving by declaring one day of the year "Drive Nice Day." The media got involved and shared the message that drivers should focus on their driving and their interactions with others for one day. The result? A period of time, longer than one day, where there were fewer incidents and collisions. In reality, a small percentage of drivers actually changed their driving habits that one day, but the collaborative and collective effect was a bigger positive result.

High-performance drivers *are* different. They care about driving and make our roads safer.

THREE SKILLS

Let's take a look at what makes a great driver on the street. The way I look at it, there are three main things you need:

- Traffic skills
- Vehicle control skills
- Mental skills

Most drivers were taught traffic skills when they got their license. That is, they learned what to do at a red light, to stop at a stop sign, what lane to make a left turn from, where you can park, what the speed limit is in a school zone, and so on.

But few were taught vehicle control skills: how to brake efficiently, how to steer to avoid something, how to control a skid, how to use vision, how to manage a vehicle to maximize its traction. Even fewer were taught the right mental skills, the right attitude, the right mindset. Most drivers are left to develop these skills and attitude through years of trial-and-error learning. Many never develop them, or make errors that lead to unfortunate results.

RISK PERCEPTION VERSUS SKILL LEVEL

Most drivers on the road today consider themselves "good" drivers. Just ask them! After all, they've earned a license that says so, right? Well, perhaps they are. But why are so many involved in crashes?

I believe that most drivers, when they first learn to drive, are taught less than half of the necessary skills they need to become "adequate" drivers (less than what

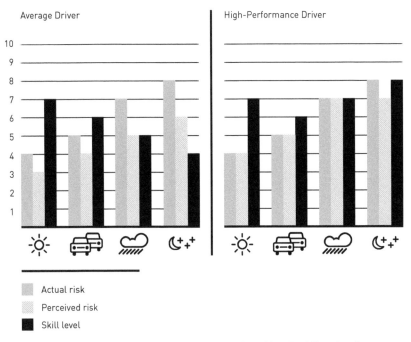

Average Driver	High-Performance Driver

Legend:
- Actual risk
- Perceived risk
- Skill level

A high-performance driver always assesses risk accurately and has the skills to handle changing conditions.

I would consider "good"). Generally, they're left to acquire good driving skills through years of trial and error (often, the "error" part in this equation leads to tragic results). This helps explain the declining crash rate with increased driver age. The more experience a driver gains, the more acquired skill, the safer the driver. But that's not the whole story.

Every time you drive, there is a certain amount of risk involved. Call this the risk level. This factor varies with changing traffic volume; road, vehicle, and weather conditions; and driver distraction/awareness. For example, driving through an intersection in rush hour in the rain has a higher risk level than a sunny drive on a wide-open country road. In the same way, driving while you're thinking about work, or eating, or tuning the stereo all cause a higher risk level than when you're focused on driving.

How a driver assesses this risk level is the most important factor. For many, the perceived risk level is lower than the real risk level. In other words, the driver's perception often doesn't represent an accurate assessment of the risks they face in the driving conditions.

Say you're driving 70 miles per hour in a 60-mile-per-hour zone in the pouring rain at night. Most people would think nothing of this situation. On a scale of 1 to 10, the driver perceives the risk level to be at 5, when in reality—accounting for the condition of the tires on the car, the amount of water on the road, the lack

Be honest and accurate with the way you assess the level of risk when driving.

of visibility, the driver's awareness level, traffic volume, and so on—the real risk level may be an 8.

Now, consider the driver's skill level. A driver may be very skilled—an 8—at driving in good conditions; but through lack of training and experience, he or she may be unskilled—a 4—at dealing with rain and darkness. With this in mind, our scenario may represent a formula for disaster. If, on that same scale of 1 to 10, the driver's skill level is a 4 in this situation, the only thing keeping the driver from a crash may be good old luck. If the driver doesn't crash, would you say they were a "good" driver, or just fortunate?

What happens when the perceived risk level encourages the driver to motor down the street or highway faster, or with less care and focus than the real risk level suggests; beyond what the driver's skill level can handle (especially if they "meet" someone in the same situation)? All too often, a crash!

The ultimate goal of all drivers, then, is to have a skill level above a matching perceived and real risk level. With this, a driver will always have a margin for error, and therefore the chance of being involved in a collision will be extremely rare.

Being a good high-performance driver is not just a matter of increasing your skill level through experience. You also need to improve your ability to accurately assess risk levels. Of course, experience can also help—as long as you have an open mind.

What's the solution? We could continue to build up both skill levels and accurate risk level assessment through years and years of experience. Unfortunately, as the crash rates suggests, a lot of people are going to be injured, or even killed, with this trial-and-error learning.

The best solution is for drivers to acquire the knowledge and skills they need through a well-designed, professionally executed advanced driver training program.

A good advanced driver training program involves real hands-on training, not just sitting in a classroom watching videos. As anyone with this experience will attest, it does far more than improve a driver's skill level. Advanced driver training gives a driver a much more accurate understanding and assessment of the risk levels involved in driving. In other words, a well-trained driver sees the perceived risk level equal with the real risk level. Many graduates of advanced driver training schools say they never realized just how close they had come to losing control of their cars before. Once they see it, they drive slower and with more control.

Unfortunately, many advanced driver training programs—high-performance driver education (HPDE) schools—are not designed and run well. They may teach vehicle control skills, but they can give drivers more confidence without addressing mental skills or mindset. This can lead to a bad situation: even if a driver has great skills, being overconfident can be just as dangerous as driving with lesser skills. It may be even more dangerous, because the driver may be prone to driving faster, with the potential for crashing at a higher speed.

How do we get people to take this very necessary training? Ask one hundred people on the street whether they "need" it, and I doubt if more than a few would say "yes." As we saw earlier, just because you've never had a collision before, that doesn't necessarily mean you're a "good" driver. But, unless you have an accurate assessment of risk levels *and* good skill levels, you're bound to have a collision soon—too soon for some.

THERE ARE NO ACCIDENTS

Have you noticed something about the language in the previous sections? I've never used the word "accident" (other than one time where I wanted to make a point). That's because an accident is "an unavoidable act of fate." A meteor falling out of the sky and crushing your car is an act of fate. Two cars crashing into each other is not.

There is a movement within our high-performance driving world, one that you can help promote: eliminate the use of the word "accident" when describing a crash.

As soon as we use "accident," we take some sense of responsibility away from the driver or drivers involved. "It was an accident. There was nothing I could do." Remember my comments about taking responsibility for what happens when we're driving, no matter whose fault it is. When we take responsibility for our actions—even for what others do—we reduce the number and severity of crashes. And that's not a bad thing.

Join the "There are No Accidents" movement! High-performance drivers take responsibility for their actions, whether they're at fault or not. And they're committed to changing the way others drive by using the proper language.

SPEED SECRET

Help change the world by eliminating the use of the word "accident" to describe car crashes.

2 VEHICLE DESIGN AND DRIVER/SAFETY AIDS

The vehicles we'll drive in the future will be more technologically advanced, with more and more safety-, convenience-, and efficiency-focused devices and aids. The challenge in writing this book is how to keep it relevant for years to come. In some ways, I have to keep the descriptions of the various driver and safety aids generic to ensure what I write isn't outdated before it's printed. Fortunately, you don't need to know the exact details of how one manufacturer's stability control system, for example, works differently from another's. No, what you need is the basics of how they work, and more importantly, how to either use them, or understand the limitations they might put on your driving.

Many automotive engineers believe we're close to a point where all the major systems have been invented already. What will change significantly over the next decades is the sensitivity of these systems. The technology needed for a self-driving car is already available, and it's just a matter of fine-tuning the technology and dealing with legislation in individual countries.

High-performance drivers are most interested in fine-tuning these systems, while automotive engineers focus constantly on developing driver aids to achieve a feeling that inspires confidence. Engineers also try to make these aids feel natural, not something that takes away from the driver's connection to the vehicle. The best systems work *with* the driver, encouraging the correct reaction at the right time.

As an example, early anti-lock braking systems (ABS) were crude when compared with today's systems. When you applied the brakes hard with first-generation ABS, the pedal would pulse dramatically. You could feel almost every one of the pulses, resulting in many drivers releasing pressure on the pedal at exactly the wrong time. In today's ABS brakes, you feel a gentle pulse. It's more sensitive, as they have gone from the brakes pulsing a few times per second to dozens of times per second. They almost invite a driver to push harder on the pedal and let the system do the hard work.

The same can be said for stability control. When a car went into even the hint of a slide, early systems would literally take over from the driver. It was as though the car was slapping your hands, saying, "You don't know what you're doing—I'm taking over." Many of today's high-end systems are much more subtle, almost to the point where it's difficult to tell when stability control is engaged.

If I walk toward you on a sidewalk, and we don't see each other because we're both looking down at our smartphones, we have to adjust our paths dramatically to avoid colliding. That's a lot like the early ABS, traction control, stability control, and adaptive cruise control systems. They detected a problem late, and then had to make large adjustments.

Now imagine us not looking at our phones, but instead seeing each other half a block away. The adjustment we would need to make in our path to not bump into each other would be very subtle, and that's what the later systems do—and future systems will be even better.

With that in mind, in this chapter I provide an overview of how these driver and safety aids work. Later, I'll discuss their use and limitations. In other words, we'll get into what specific skills you require to use, or not use, the most common systems we find in vehicles.

Before we dive in, let's take a quick look at the difference between passive and active safety.

PASSIVE AND ACTIVE SAFETY

Which would you rather do? Crash into something—but be saved from injury by seat belts, air bags, crush zones, and the overall structural strength of your vehicle—or avoid the collision altogether? That's a pretty easy decision, isn't it?

But if you can't avoid the collision, you want all of those safety devices to protect you. That's what automakers call "passive safety," what you rely on "in case of an emergency," when a collision is inevitable.

What about the devices you use to avoid the collision in the first place? That's what is known as "active safety."

While active safety systems are typically thought of as ABS, traction and stability control, automatic braking, adaptive cruise control, and lane detection, anything that helps a driver avoid hitting something or losing control of their vehicle is part of that package. Suspension design can be considered part of active safety, as a car that handles better will help you control it or be able to avoid a collision more often. Better tires are part of active safety, since they provide better traction. The same can be said for more effective braking systems. If your car will stop in less distance than another vehicle, that's better active safety.

ABS

Anti-lock braking systems have been around for a long time, so that's where we'll start. Some drivers reading this may never have driven a vehicle without ABS, while some will recall what life before ABS was like.

Imagine driving down a road in a car without ABS. A car pulls out from a driveway directly into your path, and there's no room to steer to avoid it. Your only option is to try to stop before hitting it broadside. You stomp on the brake pedal as hard as you can, in full panic mode, and the wheels lock up (that is, they stop rotating). You skid. If you've experienced locked-up brakes, you know what happens:

- You have little to no directional control over your car. With the front tires not rotating, it doesn't matter what you do with the steering wheel, as it won't change the direction of the car. For the steering to work, the front tires need to rotate.
- Your stopping distance increases, taking more time to stop than if you were to brake at the very limit, or threshold, just before the tires locked up and started skidding. (There are rare times when locking up the brakes and skidding will result in a shorter stopping distance, but these situations—on loose gravel or some amount of snow where a wedge of gravel/snow builds up in the front of the tires—are the exceptions to the rule. In most driving situations, skidding tires will result in more distance to stop the car.)

It's for these two reasons that high-performance and race drivers have been taught to "threshold brake" for so many years. Since many race and track cars do not have ABS, this valuable technique continues to be taught and practiced. (I'll discuss this more in Chapter 8.)

How does ABS work? The simplest way to look at this is to imagine that each wheel on your car has a small electronic eye, watching it turn, or rotate. If you apply so much pressure on the brake pedal that it causes one or more of the wheels to stop rotating, the eye notices and reports it to a small computer, which tells the system to release some of the pressure that you've applied. In a fraction of a second, the pressure is reapplied, then released, reapplied, released, essentially pulsing the brakes. The latest generations of ABS effectively pulse this way dozens of times per second, which is why you feel a slight movement on the pedal.

The advantages of ABS are that, by keeping the front tires rotating, you can still steer to avoid something while braking heavily, and the overall distance it takes to stop is less than if you locked up and skidded. Both of these are huge advantages to all drivers.

Using ABS is simple, too: apply the brakes hard—very hard, often harder than you think—and let the system do the work for you. When I say apply the brakes hard, I mean it. Far too many drivers, when faced with an emergency on the street, do not apply the brakes hard enough. And here's the thing: with ABS, you can't apply the brakes too hard. Imagine the effort that a weightlifter puts into raising a heavy weight in a leg press. That's the kind of pressure you need to apply on the brake pedal.

As with practically everything, there's a limit to what ABS can do. For sure, it can't go against the laws of physics. If you're using all of your tires' traction for braking, and you want to steer around a corner or object, you may have to ease off the brakes just a tiny bit. We'll have more to say about this in Chapter 10, but keep in mind that ABS does have some limits.

One final comment on ABS: it *can* stop your car in less distance than if you locked up your brakes and skidded to a stop. But what about how it compares to very skillful braking right at the limit of traction, just before the brakes lock up in a vehicle without ABS? With practice on a known surface, a skilled driver can stop in slightly less distance *without* ABS than with it. In real life, however, drivers rarely know the exact limits of traction a road surface possesses—until it's too late. And that's why, at least 95 percent of the time, a driver is better off relying on the vehicle's ABS to sense and react to a road surface's traction limits.

TRACTION CONTROL

Traction control (TC) limits the amount of slip that tires experience on the road, especially when driving on slippery surfaces like wet, snowy, or ice-covered roads.

When the driving tires—such as the rear tires on a rear-wheel-drive (RWD) car—start to slip or spin, this reduces a car's forward motion. Anyone who's driven in snow or ice knows the feeling all too well.

The same electronic eye that's watching the wheels' lack of rotation for the ABS also watches for excessive speed or rotation of a wheel. In the example of a RWD car, if the rear tires spin at some percentage faster than the front tires are, it means that rather than driving the car forward, they're spinning due to lack of traction. And an interesting thing happens when a tire is slipping or spinning excessively: it has less traction than one that is not.

This is where TC comes in: when the electronic eye reports to the computer that the rear tires are rotating faster than the front ones, the computer does something about it. There are differences between systems and how the various automakers tune these systems, but most do one or both of the following to control wheel spin:

- Reduce engine output, either by reducing the amount of throttle the engine is given by the driver—essentially, overriding the effect of the driver pushing down on the gas pedal—by changing the engine ignition or fuel injection timing, the valve timing, and/or some combination of these.
- Pulse the brakes on one or more wheels to slow the rotation or spinning of the tire.

In most conditions, TC provides the best balance between wheelspin and forward movement. In rare situations—such as with just the right (or wrong) amount of snow—a little more slip from the tires allows the car to move just enough, often enough to allow the car to roll back, then accelerate forward again. It rolls back and forth like this, eventually rocking you out of the snow. Having TC on in cases like this won't help you, which is why automakers provide a method (usually a switch or a setting) for turning TC off.

STABILITY CONTROL

Using many of the same controls as ABS and TC, stability control (SC) is designed to keep the car from skidding or spinning out of control. (It's abbreviated generically as SC, although every manufacturer has their own nomenclature for it, such as DSC, ESC, PDS, and so on.)

We'll discuss what causes a car to skid or spin later, but the most obvious reason is that the car is moving too fast for the amount of traction on the road surface. Simple, right?

SC uses the same electronic eyes that watch the speed of the rotating wheels for ABS and TC, combined with something called a "yaw sensor." This controls the amount a car is allowed to yaw.

What is yaw? Look directly down on a car as it's traveling on a straight road—on a compass, it would be heading directly north, 90 degrees from the horizontal. If the car hits a patch of ice and rotates from the 90-degree heading, and its direction now changes to a heading of 87 degrees, it has yawed. In this case, there are 3 degrees of yaw. High-performance drivers call this "rotating the car," when it's done in a more deliberate manner in a corner, rather than hitting an unexpected patch of black ice.

How does SC manage yaw? Again, every system is slightly different, but most use some combination of engine-power reduction, and especially the controlled application of some braking to one or more of the wheels. More sophisticated systems may adjust the vehicle's differential to transfer power from one wheel to another. In our example, where the car has yawed to the right by 3 degrees, the system could apply some braking to the left-rear wheel, therefore "tugging" the car back to a more straight-ahead path.

In Chapter 12, we'll discuss the limitations of stability control, and the situations in which you might want to deactivate it.

ADAPTIVE CRUISE CONTROL

Adaptive cruise control is one of the main devices used in an autonomous vehicle. This is what automatically controls the distance between it and other vehicles.

The function is quite simple: a radar or camera determines the distance between the vehicle and anything in front of it, then adjusts speed to maintain a programmed adequate distance. Behind the scenes, the details of what is "adequate" and how the speed is adjusted (engine-power adjustment, brake application) are not so simple.

EMERGENCY BRAKING SYSTEMS

Emergency braking systems use adaptive cruise control to an extreme extent. When the distance between a vehicle and something else is reducing at a rapid rate, the system automatically applies the brakes, in the equivalent of a full ABS stop.

EMERGENCY BRAKE-FORCE DISTRIBUTION

Emergency brake-force distribution (EBD) detects the speed at which a driver applies the brakes and determines whether it's a sign of potential emergency braking. If it thinks the application of the brakes indicates an emergency, it will apply even more pressure. The reason? As I mentioned earlier, many drivers do not brake hard enough. This feature is a way for automakers to make up for driver inexperience by enhancing the emergency braking—it's applying more force, quickly.

LANE DETECTION

Lane detection offers a warning system that tells the driver the vehicle is drifting out of its lane. It uses the same radar and/or cameras that adaptive cruise control uses, and compares the vehicle's position with the fog, center, and verge lines painted on roadways. Even more sophisticated systems will also compare your vehicle's path to that of others on the road. If the system detects that the vehicle has moved out of its lane or ideal path (without a turn signal being activated), a lane detection system will tug the steering wheel back towards where the system knows the vehicle should be.

DRIVE WHEELS AND ENGINE POSITION

While not technically a driver or safety system, which wheels are the driven ones, and how the weight is distributed in your car (which is greatly affected by the position of the engine), do have a big impact on the handling. A car that handles better is a safer car because it makes incidents on the road easier to avoid. There are a few key concepts you'll need to understand as we go deeper into the art of high-performance driving.

First, regardless of whether your car is rear-wheel drive (RWD), front-wheel drive (FWD), or all-wheel drive (AWD), the laws of physics apply. The differences in driving techniques covered in this book are no different, unless I specifically point them out.

The relevant laws of physics here are those that relate to weight transfer. Chapter 8 will provide more detail on this; for now, just remember that it doesn't matter what wheels are driving your car.

Where the engine is located has some impact on the dynamic weight transfer when driving. Think of holding a dumbbell above your head with one hand; each end has a weight of 10 pounds. You hold it, twist your arm as you rotate it one direction, then stop the rotation and rotate the dumbbell back in the other direction. It isn't hard to imagine that, with so much weight at the ends of the dumbbell, the effort to stop the twist and change direction is significant.

Now imagine sliding those 10-pound weights in toward the center of the dumbbell's mid-bar until they touch your hand on either side. Again, twist your arm and rotate the bar in one direction, stop it, rotate it back in the other direction, then back the other way. With the weights located closer to the center, it's easier to change the direction of the twisting, right?

The same concept applies to cars. If the weight is located at the far ends of the vehicle's chassis, it's harder to get it to change direction, whether from a straight line into a corner or from a corner in one direction to one in the opposite direction. But if the car's weight is concentrated more at the center, it's easier to change direction. That's why race cars are built with much of their weight concentrated in the center of the car.

LIMITATIONS

There's no doubt that all of the available controls and systems make driving safer. It's important to remember that they can have downsides, limitations, as well.

For example, some automakers have essentially overcome less-than-ideal chassis design or suspension design with electronics. In other words, the basic suspension design does not lead to great handling, and yet, with stability control the car will do amazing things. It feels like it handles as well as any car in the world, but that's only because the computers are controlling yaw, traction, selective powering of the wheels, and maybe even the steering. When you drive with the systems on, this isn't an issue—but think of what would happen if you turned SC off. That's why we should be mindful of the benefits and limitations of using this technology, something we'll cover in Chapter 12.

The second downside of the technology is that it encourages many drivers to become complacent (or even wildly over-confident) on the road. After all, they can make a vehicle go around a corner very fast and feel completely in control, when it's the safety systems that are controlling things. Add in the distractions that come with other forms of technology (texting, email, entertainment systems) and there's no wonder that, despite safer vehicles, the number of crashes on our highways each year are not reduced as much as they could be.

Understand how the driver and safety aids work, how you can use them, and their limitations. Most importantly, never forget that the most important system in the car is you, the driver. Until you're simply riding in an autonomous vehicle, drive within the limits. In fact, manage them—you'll learn more about how to do this in the next chapters.

3 VISION: LEADING THE WAY

Unless you're riding in a fully autonomous vehicle, what you do with your eyes is critical to driving.

If you were hearing impaired, could you drive a car at speed? Sure. It would be more difficult, but you could do it.

If you had absolutely no feeling, no sense of g-force or balance, could you drive at speed? Again, you could, but it would be more difficult—much like driving a car in a video game with no kinesthetic feedback.

Could you drive a car if you were blind? For a very short distance, right?! This points out the importance of your vision when driving. That's not to say that your auditory and kinesthetic (touch, feel, sensing g-forces, balance) senses don't play a big role in driving. In fact, your hearing processes information much faster than your vision does, so it plays a big role in sensing whether you're driving your car at the limit—it provides much of the "feel for driving at the limit."

You use your vision to get around the track or to reach your destination in street driving. But it's your kinesthetic and auditory senses that really help you drive at or near the limits. Because you can't drive at or near the limit without knowing where you're going, though, let's start with vision. After all, it's still the number one sense you use when driving.

Vision isn't just about having 20/20 eyesight (corrected or not). That—the part that is measured by reading an eye chart—is called your central vision acuity. It's what you can see with clarity directly in front of you. But, as you know, much of what happens when you're driving isn't directly in front of you. In fact, it's your peripheral vision, your depth perception, contrast sensitivity, and your ability to notice fine movement—combined with your central vision acuity—that I mean by "vision." It's an overall package.

Your vision is what gets you where you want to go, and it plays a role in sensing the limits of your car. While your auditory and kinesthetic senses tell you whether your tires are at or near their limits of grip (which allows you to drive faster where it's safe to do so), your vision helps. For example, if your car begins to slide, it will rotate; your visual picture of the horizon (if you look far enough ahead) changes.

LOOK AHEAD

Look far ahead. That's the central piece of advice that every driver, at any level, can never hear enough. More important than hearing it, though, is actually practicing it.

Look far ahead and where you want your car to go.

On the street, often driving in traffic, we develop a habit of looking at the bright shiny taillights of the vehicle in front of us. We even use this same habit if we're driving on a racetrack. Looking where the car in front of you would be in the street is not far enough to prepare for what's coming up ahead at speed on a track. What you must do is use "high aim vision," looking as far ahead of you as you can.

If you think back to when you first drove a car on a busy street, or the first time you drove on a track, you probably experienced visual overload. You couldn't process all the information coming into your brain fast enough. Over time, though, your brain learned to prioritize things, ignore the unimportant sensory cues, and focus on what should be focused on. You began looking farther ahead. When we first begin driving, there seems to be some kind of survival instinct to curl up in a ball and hide, a response that goes for our vision as well: we look to the objects immediately in front of us. When we do that, things come into our vision more quickly, leading to overload.

With experience, we look farther ahead, allowing more time for our brains to process the information around us. But our eyes, our bodies, and our brains were never really designed to move at a 100-plus miles per hour. Perhaps in a few thousand years we will have evolved (come on, Darwin!) in a way for driving to be more natural. In the meantime, we need to push our instincts and re-program our brains. We need to make looking far ahead a habit.

How? By practicing: on the street and on the track. Hey, even remind yourself to look farther ahead when walking, running, or cycling. All the time. The more you remind yourself, "Eyes up—look ahead," the more you'll build a habit for it.

SPEED SECRET

Eyes up—look ahead.

Overdriving your vision is a nasty no-no. On a street or highway, it's easy to do, especially in conditions that restrict your vision (night, rain, fog). A high-performance driver knows when to slow down and drive at a speed where there will be time to react and stop within the distance he or she can see.

It's a little bit different when driving on a track, since you know where the track goes. Still, if you can't keep up visually, slow down. Most often, that doesn't mean you have to slow very much—even a few miles per hour can make the difference. Perhaps an even better solution, though, is to remind yourself, "Eyes up—look ahead." Yes, look farther ahead.

Looking farther ahead also leads to driving more smoothly. Instead of reacting to things and making changes in direction at the very last second, you will have time to plan out your route—a smooth one. If you ever notice yourself weaving slightly from side to side within your lane, look farther ahead. Or if you find your path from one corner to the next is not as straight and smooth a line as possible, look farther ahead.

This is something you should remind yourself constantly, especially if you often drive in rush-hour traffic. In stop-and-go street driving, you may develop a habit of staring at the taillights of the car in front of you. Try looking up the roadway as far as you can see, scanning the distance in between with your peripheral vision.

By constantly reminding yourself to look farther ahead, you'll build a good vision habit.

Is it possible to look *too far ahead*? How far ahead should you be looking? I don't think a driver can ever look too far ahead. On the track, if you can't see all the way around the track and see your own taillights, then look farther ahead! Obviously, that's an exaggeration, but that should be your thought.

When driving on the street, the recommended distance to look ahead is measured in time: it should be in the 12-to-15-second range (I recommend 15 seconds). That is, notice an object up ahead and begin counting, "One-one-thousand, two-one-thousand, three-one-thousand . . . ," until you get to fifteen-one-thousand. That's when you should be just passing that object. If you get to the object before you count to fifteen-one-thousand, then you're not looking far enough ahead. Pick your vision up and check again.

This method of checking how far ahead you're looking isn't something you should do once and then never revisit. Make a habit of checking how far ahead you're looking every now and then, at different speeds. Each time you look farther ahead, say to yourself, "Eyes up—look ahead." When you do that, you're building a good habit while also developing a trigger phrase to remind yourself. Eventually, you'll simply say, "Eyes up—look ahead," and you'll habitually look farther ahead.

SCAN

You don't want to simply stare a long distance ahead. You need to scan, forward and back, and side to side, while most of the time of time looking way ahead. As you approach a corner, you want to look well through it, glancing quickly back to where you'll start to turn into it, back through the corner, back to the apex of the corner (more about this in Chapter 9), way ahead again, and so on. Keep your eyes moving, scanning.

Especially when driving on the street—but also on the track—you should have a 360-degree view around your car at all times. That requires scanning—ahead, peripherally, ahead, into the mirrors, ahead, to a point on the roadway just ahead, ahead, to the side, ahead, mirrors, and so on. Notice that the emphasis here is always on looking way ahead, but you should never be surprised by another car behind or to the side of you. Big-picture awareness is what you're after.

LOOK WHERE YOU WANT TO GO

Look where you want to go, not where you don't want to go. That may sound obvious, but it's not. There's a human instinct to look where we *don't* want to go—in other words, at the problem. Perhaps it's a leftover from the days when we had to identify and avoid a saber-toothed tiger. If you've ever found yourself walking along a hallway or sidewalk toward another person and ended up doing one of those "let's avoid each other" dances, you know what I mean: if you look at the person walking toward you, and that person looks at you, it's nearly impossible to not walk into each other.

This is target fixation: you know you should look where you want to go, but sometimes things happen right in front of us and our vision locks onto whatever it is. Our attention may be attracted by a car pulling out of a driveway right in front of us, or by one spinning out on the track. Instead of looking where we want to go—to either side of the car—our eyes are attracted to it and we stare at it.

SPEED SECRET

Keep your eyes moving. Scan ahead, to the sides and rear of your vehicle.

Target fixation is part of human nature: we like to look at things. Used the right way, looking where we want to go, it's a good thing. It helps you go where you want, as long as you focus your vision on where you want to go. But it can be a bad thing if you fixate on a spinning car, a tire wall off to the side of a track, a car pulling out of a driveway, a child running out from between two cars, or anything else you don't want to steer toward.

While your hands and arms turn the steering wheel, your eyes tell them where and how much to turn. Information goes through your eyes where it's processed by your brain, which tells your arms and hands what to do. If the information going into your brain indicates a path or direction to the left, your arms and hands will turn the wheel to the left.

You've probably had the experience of looking at something along the side of the road, then noticed that your car was drifting in that direction. If you look there, you'll steer there. That's why it's so important to focus on where you want to go, not on where you don't want to go.

Try it for yourself. Without your car moving, while seated behind the wheel, look to the right and try to turn the steering wheel to the left. Pretty awkward, right?

If a car pulls out in front of you, where do you want to look? The correct answer is, to either side of it. If you look at it, you'll steer toward it.

Or, let's say you've made an error while driving on a track and you're sliding or spinning off the track surface. Human instinct is to look at where you're about to crash. Instead of looking at the wall you might crash into, look where you want to go—most likely back up the track. That will improve your chances of surviving the spin.

Practice this in your everyday driving. Identify a manhole cover on the roadway, then look just to the right or left of it and let your hands and arms guide your car around it. When changing lanes, focus on the gap between the lane reflectors. When pulling into a parking spot, look at the empty space, rather than the cars on either side.

What you're doing here is practicing looking at nothing. Your eyes are attracted to objects. In high-performance driving (or any driving, for that matter), you shouldn't look at

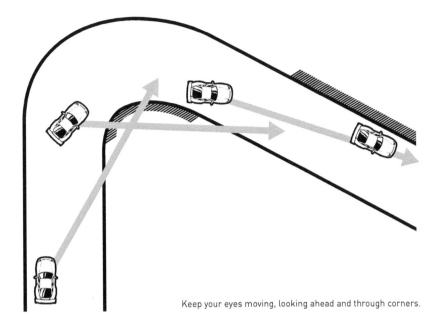

Keep your eyes moving, looking ahead and through corners.

anything at all: you should look at the gaps, the "nothing." Developing this skill alone will lead to much safer driving than nearly anything else you do.

When you want your car to follow a specific path or line through a corner, look along that path. There are rare times, especially when driving on the track, where you won't be able to see where you want to go. The path will be blocked by a hill or some other object. So not only do you have to look where you want to go—you must *imagine* where you want to go.

360-DEGREE VIEW

It's just as important to know what's behind and beside you as it is to know what's in front of you.

As a high-performance driver, you need to know where all other vehicles are around you. More than that, you want to know where they are *and* where they're going.

Fighter pilots call this ability to know what is around them at all times "situational awareness." Driving a vehicle in today's traffic requires the same level of situational awareness as

> *SPEED SECRET*
>
> **Drive with a 360-degree view around you.**

a fighter pilot or race car driver. If you're track driving, it's just as critical to know where other cars are around you.

High-performance drivers rely on their mirrors. This doesn't mean driving while staring in the mirrors: you can't drive well if you only focus on what others are doing. But you do need to use your mirrors almost constantly. If they're adjusted properly, even when your eyes are focused ahead, you can still be aware of the movement of other cars in the mirrors by using your peripheral vision. Use this technique on the street or track.

With the mirrors adjusted properly, you should have a 360-degree view of the road and traffic around you at all times. Again, another vehicle should never surprise you by "coming out of nowhere."

This is a skill that takes some practice. Don't allow yourself to get into "tunnel vision" mode. Keep your head up, look as far down the road as possible, use your peripheral vision, and keep your eyes moving. Look for the "big picture." Don't focus on any single thing, but keep track of everything around you.

Make a game of it: your goal is to know where everyone around you is at all times, to never be surprised by anyone.

As you pass someone, keep track of them in your peripheral vision and mirrors. As another vehicle comes up from behind to pass you, make note of them until they're out of sight. Learn to recognize any slight movement in the mirrors and track other vehicles and objects around you.

MIRRORS

If they're so important, how do you adjust your mirrors properly? It helps that nearly all modern cars have mirrors that can be adjusted so that there are *no* blind spots.

The first step is to adjust the rearview mirror to give you a view directly to the rear. Position it so that it covers your view straight out the rear window. Don't bother tilting it to one side or the other to give you a view of traffic on either side of your car: that's what the side mirrors are for.

Next, while sitting in your driving position, adjust the left side mirror so that you *can't* see the side of your car without tilting your head almost to the driver side window. If you're like most drivers, this means angling the mirror out much wider than you may have done in the past. Then, adjust the right side mirror so you can't see the side of the car until you tilt your head toward the center of the car. Again, this probably means angling it out wider than before.

At first, this may seem strange. You're probably used to just seeing the side of your car in those side mirrors. But think about it: you don't really need to see the side of your own car. It will never run into itself!

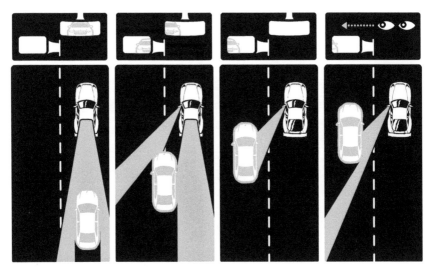

When you adjust and use your mirrors properly, you can eliminate blind spots.

By shifting out your side mirrors wider this way, you have eliminated that dreaded blind spot. In fact, the next step involves checking just that.

While driving down a two-lane road in the right lane, note a vehicle coming up to pass you from behind, in the left lane. Without moving your head, glance in the rearview mirror and follow it as it approaches your car. Just before it disappears from your view in the rearview mirror, glance to the left side mirror. There it is. Now follow it in the side mirror as it begins to pass you. Then, just before it disappears from the side mirror, you should see it with your peripheral vision.

Notice that, without even turning your head, you never had a blind spot.

Then try the same thing with the right side. Watch as you pass a vehicle traveling in the right lane go from your peripheral vision, to your right side mirror, to your rearview mirror. Again, no blind spot. If there is, your side mirror adjustment needs some fine-tuning. If the car disappears from your sight for even a fraction of a second, you have a blind spot and should adjust mirrors to compensate.

Perform this routine every time you get into a car where the mirrors haven't been adjusted by you. It only takes seconds, and it can make a big difference. You can also have a friend or family member walk all the way around your parked car while you sit in the driver's seat and note whether can see them at all times.

I've tested this method on thousands of different vehicles, and never once have I ended up with a blind spot.

Where does this leave shoulder-checking before you change lanes? It's still something you should do—kinda—but not to the point where you cannot see the traffic in front of you with your peripheral vision. Think of it as a "shoulder peek" instead of a shoulder check.

If you do the traditional shoulder check—a technique that was developed and taught in drivers education in the 1950s and not changed since, despite dramatic changes in vehicle design—there will be a fraction of a second (or more) when the blind spot is directly in front of your car. That's not good!

Instead, try a "shoulder peek," looking almost directly into the side mirror (the one that you trust to tell you whether there is another vehicle next to you now that is adjusted properly). Your peripheral vision will be peeking over your shoulder while it's also "keeping an eye" on what's directly in front of you.

It may take a little while to feel comfortable not seeing your own car in the side mirrors (if you really need to see it now and then, just tilt your head a little). Also, you may need to train yourself to stop relying on the side mirrors for looking to the rear. And it may take a couple of weeks to get used to the position of the side mirrors. But once you do, I guarantee you'll be much more comfortable and confident in traffic.

An added bonus to this mirror position? The bright headlights of vehicles following you at night won't shine directly in your eyes from the side mirrors anymore.

Please give this an honest try, even if it means adjusting the side mirrors outward a little each day. I promise, you won't go back.

Most driving experts will say you should check your mirrors every five to seven seconds. Although this is a good, basic guideline, sometimes it's too often, and sometimes it's not enough.

You should check your mirrors often enough to always know what's around you—behind and to the sides. Sometimes that means checking every five to seven seconds, sometimes less, sometimes more. On the racetrack, check them each time you enter a straightaway after exiting a corner, and give a quick glance prior to the brake zone for corners at the ends of longer straights.

The key is to get used to using the mirrors so that you don't actually have to turn toward them and look into them. Instead, it should be just a quick glance, largely using your peripheral vision. In fact, if you adjust and use your mirrors properly, you'll notice most vehicles around you in your peripheral vision, and presto: situational awareness.

Adjust and use your mirrors to ensure you're never surprised by another vehicle.

Your mirrors are a great tool for safety. If you use them properly, you'll always know whether you have an "escape route" on either side to avoid a collision in front of you. If you check them often enough, you will note other vehicles following too closely and be able to adjust your driving accordingly. You will also notice if you are holding up another vehicle behind you, giving you the option to move over and let them pass.

We all need to remind ourselves to check our mirrors, constantly. The next time you get behind the wheel, make sure you've adjusted the side mirrors properly. Then practice checking them often. It will make you feel more confident—and safer—in heavy traffic.

4 SEATING AND BODY POSITION

Here's something so basic that you probably haven't thought much about it since you first learned to drive: you'll never be able to drive well if you're not sitting properly behind the wheel.

If you've ever watched auto racing on TV, or been to a race, and had the opportunity to see the cockpit of a race car, you're familiar with the seats that race drivers use. Most have been custom-fitted for the driver, many of them specifically molded to the driver's body. At a minimum, professional race drivers will spend more than four hours making sure the seat positions their body properly. They know the importance of the ideal seating position.

The same principles apply to any high-performance driver.

Your seating position is critical to being able to control your car.

Your seat has three purposes when it comes to performance driving: supporting your body so it doesn't move around, keeping you comfortable, and ensuring you're positioned properly to use the controls (steering wheel and pedals) accurately.

Take time to set your car's seat to suit you perfectly. You may have used the same seating position for years, but that doesn't necessarily mean that it's ideal. Start by thinking about sitting *in* the seat, not *on* it. Push your butt back into the seat as far as it will go. The more of your body that's in contact with the seat, the more support you'll have, and the better you'll be able to feel what your car is doing.

Most performance cars allow you to adjust seat height. Depending on your body size, you should begin by raising or lowering the seat. I recommend aiming your eyes as close to the middle of the windshield as possible. Aim too low and you'll be straining to look up; too high, and you'll be forced to look down. It's for this second reason—and what we talked about in the previous chapter about looking far ahead—that I suggest setting the seat a little on the low end of the adjustment. This will tend to force you to look up and far ahead.

If you do any track driving, then you have to consider what it will be like when you're wearing a helmet. Some taller drivers need to have their seat mounted lower to the floor to ensure they have enough head room with a helmet on. If you modify your seat's mounting brackets to lower it, I highly recommend having a qualified person do this—I've heard of too many seats that have come loose from their mounting brackets in a crash, resulting in the driver being injured.

You must be able to depress the clutch pedal all the way to the floor without fully extending your leg. If you don't have a clutch, pretend that you do. (If you don't know what a clutch pedal is, I suggest using Google to learn what it is and where it is located!) You can also push your right foot all the way to the floor on the throttle (gas pedal) while your car is parked and turned off. With your foot pushing on either the clutch or gas pedal all the way to the floor, you should still have a bend in your knee. If you have to straighten your leg to do this, move the seat further forward. If your legs feel scrunched up—especially if they're interfering with the steering wheel or column—move the seat back.

At this point, the bottom of the seat should be fairly close to where you want it, so it's time to adjust it for your arms. Rest your wrist at the top of the steering wheel, at the 12 o'clock position. If you have to pull the back of your shoulder off the seat to do this (that is, to reach this far), you need to move the back of your seat forward, which usually means sitting more upright. Adjust your seat back so that you can place the wrist of one hand at the top of the wheel without having to pull your shoulder off the seat back.

Now, adjust the steering-wheel position, tilting it up or down and moving it closer or further away from you. For most drivers, having the wheel as low as possible, just before it begins to interfere with your legs, provides the most comfort and steering control. If the wheel is too high, it'll feel as if you have to reach more, especially as your hand goes past the top when turning.

You may be saying, "That feels weird! It's uncomfortable to be sitting that far forward and so close to the steering wheel." Get used to it. After all, the reason it feels weird and uncomfortable is because it's new and the position hasn't become familiar yet. You've made sitting too far away from the wheel a habit, which you need to break. Develop a new habit that lets you control your car better. In fact, it's your habits that make any adjustment to your seating position so difficult. As you know, it takes time to change habits, so give it time.

If you're not sitting in the proper position, you'll never drive to your potential. Since you gain much of the feel for what your car is doing through your seat and steering wheel, you need to be in the right position to take in what it's telling you.

As you adjust the tilt of the seat back, you may need to go back and fine-tune the distance between the bottom of the seat and the pedals. This can give your legs the proper clearance around the steering column while making sure you still have a bend in your legs. This is a bit of a circular process: first you adjust the bottom of the seat for leg position and overall height, then you set the tilt of the back for the ideal length from the steering wheel, then the seat bottom for steering column clearance, then seat back again, and so on. Once you think you've found the ideal position, go for a drive and see how it feels. The more different this new arrangement is from the way you've adjusted your driving position in the past, the longer it may take you to get used to it.

If your car has lumbar (lower back) support, this will also be a good time to fine-tune these features so that they provide more comfort and support. There's no real right or wrong when it comes to these adjustments—just find what provides the most lateral support and feels comfortable to you.

Once you've found and tested the ideal position, use the seat's memory button to save it, assuming your car has that option. If your car doesn't have a seat memory feature, look at your settings and note some reference points, such as how the top of the steering wheel aligns with the front of the hood, or how close

High-performance drivers know the importance of the proper seating position.

your ear is to the B-pillar. Also note how many "clicks" your seat is from the fully-forward position. This will help you quickly adjust your seating position.

Now that you're sitting properly in the seat, do everything you can to hold yourself there by using your seat belt or harnesses. Give the belt a tug and cinch it tight across your hips. Yes, it's there to save you in an impact, but before that it's there to hold you in place and support your body while braking, cornering, and accelerating. Original-equipment seat belts are okay, but proper four-, five-, or six-point harnesses are much better, both for safety and for support. If you're going to track your car for any length of time, you should probably think of investing in a harness.

If you're going to do any amount of track driving, I also strongly recommend upgrading to a high-performance seat that provides good lateral support. No matter how good your original seat is, it's not going to hold you in position like one that's designed specifically for support. Many drivers have reported that the single biggest improvement in their ability to drive fast around a track did not come from more horsepower, better tires or brakes, upgraded suspension, or anything else. It came from one simple improvement: their bodies being supported by a high-performance seat.

Now, go back and think about what I said at the beginning of this chapter and ask yourself these three questions:

1. Does my seat provide lateral support?
2. Is my seat and seating position comfortable?
3. Am I sitting in a position that allows me to consistently use the steering wheel and pedals with precision and accuracy?

Finally, now that you have your seating position sorted out, ask yourself one last, critical question: if I get in a crash, will my seat and seating position help protect me? Yes, your seat and seating position can play an important role in helping you survive a crash. No one likes to think about it happening, but it does.

5 STEERING

Like golf and many other sports, high-performance driving is a two-handed activity. You won't see a hockey player skating with just one skate, so don't rely on one hand to turn the steering wheel.

When you drive on the street, you build habits. These will show up whether you're driving on your favorite twisty highway or on the racetrack. If one of your daily habits is steering with one hand, you'll bring that with you when you perform high-performance driving. Even if you start using two hands when you get on a track, there will likely be a small part of your mental processing taken up with converting your actions from one-handed driving because it's not yet a habit.

I look at street driving as a way to build good habits for driving on the track. In other words, driving on the street is practice for high-performance driving: you can build the right track-driving habits while driving on the street, legally.

When drivers attend a high-performance driver education (HPDE) program at a racetrack, one of the key habits they must break is steering with one hand, while the other hand rests on the shifter. Start now by building good driving habits on the street.

Drive with your hands at the
9 o'clock and 3 o'clock positions.

Drive with your hands at the 9 and 3 o'clock positions on the steering wheel.

Build good driving habits by steering with two hands on the wheel at all times. If it doesn't feel completely comfortable to do this, it's because this hasn't become a habit yet. Stay focused and know that it will become your habit.

Now that you have two hands on the wheel, where should you place them? Hold the steering wheel at the 9 and 3 o'clock positions. You may need to alter those positions slightly because of your steering wheel's design, but start by gently resting your thumbs on the horizontal spokes of the wheel: this will result in your hands being as near to the 9 and 3 o'clock positions as possible.

You should be able to turn through nearly any corner you encounter without taking your hands from those positions. In very tight corners on a racetrack—or on some corners when driving on the street—you may have to loosen your grip with your hand at the bottom of the wheel as it rotates past 90 degrees, sliding the wheel through your hand, and then picking up the 9 or 3 o'clock position again as you straighten the wheel.

Ideally, you should not have to reposition your hands prior to turning into a corner, nor should you have to go hand-over-hand to turn through a corner. Keep both hands on the wheel as much as possible. After shifting with

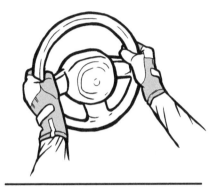

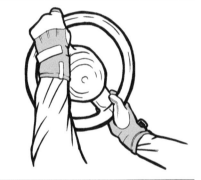

For maximum control while turning steering wheel more than 90 degrees, keep your hands in the 9 and 3 o'clock positions (possibly sliding your bottom hand when having to turn the wheel very sharply).

a stick shift, get your hand back on the wheel—there's no need to hold the shifter (it will not fall out of your car . . . and if it was about to, holding onto it is not the best fix!).

Many drivers were taught to shuffle-steer or to use the hand-over-hand method. Hey, they also taught holding the steering wheel at the 10 and 2 positions. That was good advice back when steering wheels were larger than they are now, when it often took more effort to turn the wheel (that is, before power steering) and the entire steering system wasn't as precise.

The problem with shuffle-steering is that it's not as smooth as keeping your hands at the 9 and 3 positions and simply rotating the wheel. With practice, some drivers can perform well with shuffle-steering. The very nature of the movement, though, is a series of near starts and stops of the rotation of the wheel.

The problem with hand-over-hand steering is that it's too easy to turn the wheel more than is needed. Minimum steering movement should be your goal—turn the wheel no more than is needed. Turn it just as much as you absolutely need to get through a corner, then straighten it out again as soon as possible.

Some drivers reposition their hands just prior to entering a corner. For example, in a tight right-hand corner, they place their hands at the 8 and 2 positions before the corner. This gives them more rotation before running out of room or crossing their arms while turning. While there's some validity to this thinking, it comes with at least two problems:

- Repositioning of the hands takes place just prior to the corner, while braking; that's not a good time to be moving your hands on the wheel.
- If the car should begin to slide or even spin, it's easy for you to lose track of where straight ahead is on the wheel. If your hands are always at the 9 and 3 positions, it's easy to know where straight ahead is—just straighten your arms. I've seen many spins caused by the driver not being able to get the steering pointed straight quickly enough.

Sometimes you need to turn the wheel "crisply," and other times you need to "bend" the car into a corner with a gentler, progressive rotation of the wheel. The rate or speed at which you turn the wheel is just as important as when and how much you turn it. And just to make driving that much more challenging, every corner, every car, and every situation is different. The best drivers are able to adapt the timing, rate, and amount of steering to suit different corners.

SPEED SECRET

Turn the steering wheel as little as possible, then straighten it up as soon as you can. Minimize movement of the steering wheel.

The speed at which you turn the steering wheel should be different, depending on the corner you're navigating.

You can progressively, linearly, or digressively turn the wheel. When you progressively turn the wheel, you start slow but gradually increase the speed at which you turn it. Digressive turning is the opposite: you start quickly but gradually slow down the rate at which you turn the wheel. Linear turning means that you turn the wheel at a constant speed.

Terms we use to describe the turning of the wheel include "arcing it into a corner," "bending it in," "crisply turning the wheel," and simply the "turn-in."

Be aware of how you turn the steering wheel. I recommend being aware of it when driving on the street. Do you turn the wheel exactly the same for every corner? Or do you change it up based on the radius, elevation, and camber change in the roadway, the width of the laneway, and how your car handles? You should alter your turning in each case. You can't be a great high-performance driver if you always turn the wheel the same way. Some corners plead for a gentle, bend-in, which is a slow, usually progressive, turn for fast corners. Other corners reward a quick, crisp turn-in (typically a tighter corner).

Be aware of how you turn the steering wheel the next time you drive on a racetrack. There's no need to judge whether one way is good or bad, just pay attention to what you do. Experiment with it. Play with different speeds and whether you're steering in a progressive or digressive way. During this experimentation, you'll learn what the different speeds and rates do and how they impact the way the car changes direction. Eventually, when you need the car to behave in a certain way, you'll know exactly how to make it perform, because you've practiced using different ways to turn the wheel.

Speaking of the rate that you turn the wheel, you should initiate slowly but react fast. The slower you initially turn the steering wheel, the longer your tires will grip the road or track surface. Think of it as breaking a piece of string. If you slowly pull it from both ends, it will take a lot of force to snap it; but if you quickly snap it apart, it will break with less force. That's why you want to slowly build up the tires' traction forces by slowly turning the wheel into corners. Of course, if you're too slow to turn the wheel, you'll drive off the outside of the corner (so you have to be reasonable about this!).

Once you've turned the steering wheel, if the car begins to slide, skid, or spin (the "three deadly Ss"), react quickly to catch it. Many drivers will let the car slide, thinking they've got it . . . only they don't got it! Instead, if the car begins to slide, look where you want to go and quickly steer to catch it. Initiate slowly, react quickly.

Turn the steering wheel with both hands, pushing up with one and pulling down with the other. This will give you the best leverage and fine-skill control. Remember, driving is a two-handed sport.

Think about this: turning the steering wheel is a terrible thing to do to a car. It slows the car down. When you turn the steering wheel, the front tires actually begin to scrub speed because they're at an angle to the direction you're going.

The closer you drive to the limit, the more you control the direction of the car with the weight transfer (a detail covered in Chapter 8) and the less you change direction with the steering wheel. It's at this point that you realize just how much turning the front wheels slows the car down: turning functions as a brake.

Drive a low-horsepower go kart and pay attention to how much you slow it down by turning the steering wheel. The same thing happens with your car—it's just harder to notice.

Smooth is fast. The way you hold and turn the wheel is meant to help you drive smoother. The smoother you drive, the more traction your tires will have, and the more control you'll have. You'll also be able to drive faster, more consistently, on the track (and it will be more fun driving on that favorite twisty highway).

You receive a lot of sensory information through the steering wheel, information that helps you determine if you're near, at, or over the car's limits. The steering wheel isn't just an input device: it's also an output device. You tell it what to do by turning it, but you also get feedback from it. If you hold the wheel with clenched hands, you'll notice this feedback less. Relax your hands so that you feel the vibrations and pressure back through the wheel, into your arms, and back into your brain.

SPEED SECRET

The less you turn the steering wheel, the faster you will go.

To sum up:

- Keep both hands on the wheel.
- Drive with your hands at the 9 and 3 o'clock positions.
- Use both hands and arms to turn the wheel—push up with one while pulling down with the other to rotate the wheel.
- Minimize movement of the wheel—put the least amount of steering input in, then straighten the wheel as soon as possible.
- Be aware of and use different timing, rates, and amounts of wheel rotation to suit the situation.
- Be smooth.

Lastly, to reinforce what we covered in Chapter 3, the car goes where you look. It's your vision that drives what you do with the steering wheel. Eyes up and look way ahead, to where you want the car to go. Do that, and your hands—and the steering wheel—will follow.

Ah, footwork. This is where the magic of performance driving takes place. Because it's so hard to see—and we're rarely able to witness the dance performed by the best drivers—this part of driving often gets overlooked and overshadowed by things like the cornering line. But what you do with your feet may have a bigger role in how fast and controlled you're able to drive than anything else. Without great footwork, you won't be able to drive your car at or near its limit on the line you want to drive through corners.

There are either three or four pedals in every car:

1. Throttle (gas pedal)—Always. At least for now, all vehicles have a throttle to control acceleration. In electric cars, this is called the accelerator.

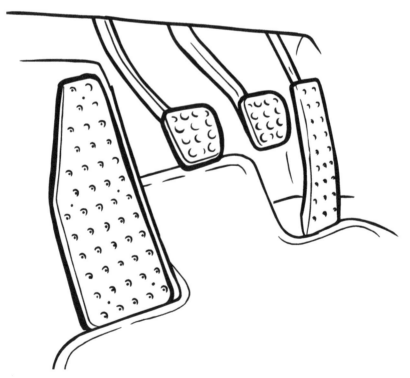

High-performance drivers use the pedals—throttle, brake, clutch (if equipped with one), and dead pedal—with finesse.

2. Brake pedal—Always. For now and the foreseeable future of vehicles that we control, there will be a brake pedal to control deceleration.
3. Dead pedal—Always. You may not have ever heard of the dead pedal before. It's that area where you should place your left foot to brace and support your body. In most cars, there's a pad for your foot to rest on. Although we call it a pedal, it doesn't move. Place your left foot on it and keep it there all the time when you're not actually depressing or releasing the clutch pedal (in manual vehicles), or using the brake pedal (more about this option later). The support you gain when you place your left foot on the dead pedal will make a positive difference in your driving.
4. Clutch pedal—Sometimes, depending on whether your car has a manual transmission or not.

The use of the throttle, brake, and clutch (when there is one) is directly related to controlling your car's speed and traction. As I mentioned, the dead pedal plays a big role in providing the support you need to sense what your car is doing. Later chapters will discuss how using these pedals can affect your car's balance—and how fast you're able to drive. For now, we'll take a quick look at each to cover all the basics.

First, we should consider your footwork generally. The key words here are "smooth," "precise," "deliberate," and "quick." Think of the footwork a great dancer uses and you'll get the idea of how a great driver's footwork operates.

There was a time when high-performance drivers were taught to think of applying the throttle and brake pedals as though they were squeezing an orange—or even like there was an egg between your foot and the pedals. That was in the day when cars had relatively low levels of traction and low performance levels. Today's cars are so much more capable that your initial application of the pedals can—and should—be crisper and even harder, but still smooth.

That's not to say that you shouldn't be smooth when applying or releasing the pedals. You must be. But in a deliberate way.

Hold your non-dominant hand open, fingers gently spread. Think of this as your throttle or brake pedal. With your dominant hand, make a fist, and think of it as your foot about to apply pressure to the throttle or brake. First, hold your fist about 6 inches away from your open hand, then punch it. Notice the smacking sound when your fist hits your other hand. That's not smooth.

Be smooth, precise, deliberate, and quick with your use of the pedals.

Now hold your fist about a quarter of an inch away from the other hand. As quick and as hard as you can, push your fist into the open hand. Notice the difference in sound. That's the difference between being smooth and not smooth. You probably applied the same amount of force, or pressure, to your open hand in both scenarios. In the second approach, though, it was smoother. That's what being smooth and deliberate means.

Being precise and quick has more to do with how you move your feet on the pedals. If you're moving your right foot from the throttle to the brake pedal, it needs to happen as quickly as possible, and it should hit the same spot on the pedal each time—that's the precision you need.

THROTTLE

The throttle is not an on-off switch; it's meant to be used progressively, down and up. Sometimes you'll squeeze it down very quickly, and other times you'll gently and slowly depress it. Sometimes you'll release the throttle quickly, and other times you'll come off it slowly. Sometimes you'll modulate the throttle through a corner, smoothly and gently, to change the car's balance and speed (more about this later).

As a general rule, when it's time to begin braking for a corner, your release of the throttle should be crisp and quick. When you're releasing the throttle in the middle of a corner, to manage a slide or mistake you've made, it should be done gently and smoothly. This is called "breathing the throttle." This concept relates to a gentle easing off of the throttle, rather than a complete and relatively quick lift off it.

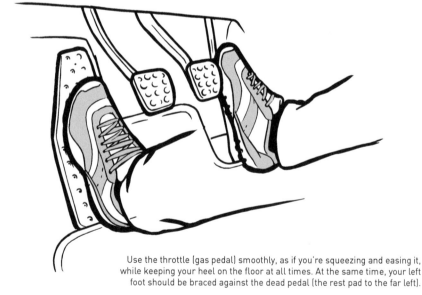

Use the throttle (gas pedal) smoothly, as if you're squeezing and easing it, while keeping your heel on the floor at all times. At the same time, your left foot should be braced against the dead pedal (the rest pad to the far left).

When you begin accelerating out of a corner, your goal should be to progressively squeeze the pedal down to full throttle without ever easing up on it. In other words, you shouldn't push down on the gas pedal, ease back up, and down again. You want to begin squeezing down on the throttle at a time and rate that allows you to continuously push down on it until you're at full throttle. That's the goal.

Since we're all human, and we make mistakes every now and then, you may begin accelerating too early or too quickly. When you do, you'll find that you need to ease up on the throttle to avoid running off the edge of the road or track. As long as you ease up gently and smoothly—breathe the throttle—that's okay. It would be better if you didn't do this, but if you're correcting for an error you made, just be smooth.

In Chapter 8, I'll discuss managing your car's weight transfer. For now, understand that you use the throttle for more than accelerating. It also changes and manages the balance of your car, which impacts how it handles, as well as how you control a skid or slide.

It may seem obvious, but be sure you're keeping your right heel on the floor when using the throttle. It's less tiring, more comfortable, and, as we'll see in a moment, it's part of how you should use the brake pedal.

BRAKE PEDAL

Brake with the ball of your foot pushing on the pedal, as that's the strongest and most sensitive part of your foot. You'll feel the pedal better when you brake this way.

Be sure to keep your heel on the floor. If you're also braking with your right foot, your heel should rarely or barely move from its position on the floor. With it in position, you can operate the throttle and brake by simply pivoting your foot between the two pedals.

Having said that, I know it's a challenge for some drivers to keep their heel on the floor while using the ball of their foot to press on the brake pedal. Some cars' brake pedals are a little too high for someone with a smaller foot to reach.

In this case, you have two options: either compromise by lifting your foot a little to reach the pedal or modify your car. If you're going to modify your car, be absolutely sure you work with someone who knows what they're doing to make the changes. The floor could be raised slightly, but the challenge is to do that without having any chance of something jamming the throttle down.

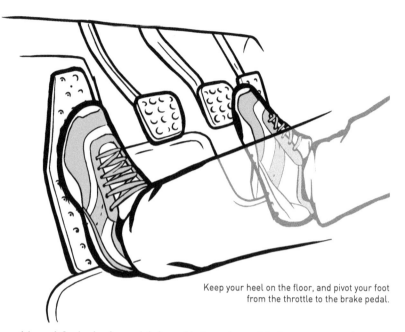

Keep your heel on the floor, and pivot your foot from the throttle to the brake pedal.

You could modify the brake pedal, but this is such a critical component that I don't recommend doing this unless you have someone who is extremely knowledgeable at engineering the changes, along with the right fabricator. Imagine what would happen if the brake pedal was to bend or break because of incorrect modifications.

The way most drivers brake when driving on the street is to apply the brake pedal gently, and then gradually increase the pressure as they get closer to whatever they're stopping for—a traffic light, stop sign, traffic, or whatever. That's not how high-performance drivers brake. In fact, it's the opposite.

One of my mantras is "smooth is fast," and it's true. Smooth use of the pedals and steering wheel is what makes the difference between a good and a bad performance driver. But you can be too smooth with the initial application of the brakes.

Your initial application of the brake pedal should be smooth but hard. You want to get to the maximum pressure that you're going to use as quickly as you can. Then, when the timing is right, you should gently ease off the brakes.

Each time you brake, there is a braking zone—the time and distance you travel from when you initially apply the brakes to the point where your foot comes completely off the pedal. Think of it this way: you want to do two-thirds of your braking in the first one-third of the braking zone. That isn't entirely accurate, but it's a good image of how you should use the brakes.

I should be clear about one thing: practically every brake zone is different. For this reason, the amount of pressure you apply initially, how long you hold maximum pressure, and how gradually you release it will vary almost every time

SPEED SECRET

The initial application and subsequent release of the brakes is what separates the best drivers from the rest.

you brake. At least that's the way it is when driving on a track. How you brake when you come to a stop at a traffic light might be similar each time, but there's a big difference when it comes to slowing for corners on a track or on a twisty highway road.

That is the biggest difference between braking on the street and on the track. On the street you're often (but not always) braking to come to a stop, whereas on the track you're simply slowing the car for a corner. On the track, you can think of braking, and the braking zone, as a speed adjustment.

With the initial application and release of the brakes covered (for now), let's talk about the physical act of pressing down on the brake pedal, with either your right or left foot.

Should you brake with your right or left foot? Great question! There are pros and cons to both approaches, and often it's your car that will dictate which foot you use. Let's take a look.

In some cars, it's nearly impossible to left-foot-brake, because your left foot is being used to operate the clutch. If you drive a manual transmission car that requires the use of the clutch, all you can really do is use your left foot to brake in corners where you don't have to downshift, when you don't need to use the clutch.

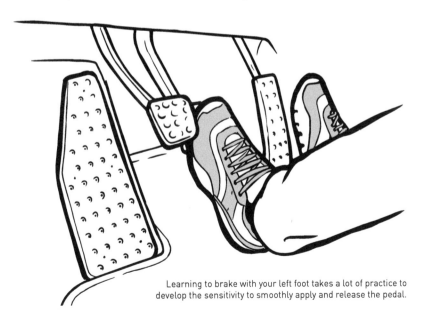

Learning to brake with your left foot takes a lot of practice to develop the sensitivity to smoothly apply and release the pedal.

Here's one of the cons of using this method: because your left foot is habituated to using the clutch—which doesn't require much finesse when depressing it (although it does when releasing it)—when you go to operate the brake pedal with your left foot, you often end up over-slowing. And that's the best-case scenario. The worst-case scenario is that you almost launch yourself into the windshield. If you've tried left-foot-braking, or you recall the first time you did it, you know what I'm talking about. Your left foot doesn't have the finesse and sensitivity that your right foot has, because your right foot is constantly modulating the gas pedal, developing very fine motor skills.

Should you use left-foot-braking, then? The answer can best be summed up with this statement: a good right-foot-braker will drive better than a mediocre left-foot-braker.

Unless you have the opportunity to fully develop your left-foot-braking skills, then leave it alone. You'll likely be better off sticking to right-foot-braking.

What are the benefits of left-foot-braking? The ability to eliminate the time it takes to move your right foot from the throttle to the brake pedal, and even—in some, I'd say, rare cases—the ability to overlap braking and throttle at the same time. (This is an advanced technique, and it can often cause more harm than good; some new vehicles will sense this and assume the worst, to the point where they shut the engine power down.)

When a driver is looking for the last few tenths of a second of lap time around a racetrack, eliminating the transition time from throttle to brakes, and brakes to throttle, can make the difference. But is that you? Are you looking to save that last few tenths of a second off your lap times?

If you're driving an automatic or semiautomatic transmission car, your left foot is just along for the ride, since it's not being used to operate the clutch. In this case, why not use both feet, right foot on the throttle, left foot on the brakes? With enough use and training, you can develop great finesse and sensitivity with your left foot.

There are still a few cons with left-foot-braking worth mentioning, if only for the purpose of making you aware enough of them so that you don't do these:

- When driving at or near the limits of your car, your body must counteract the g-force just to hold it in position. A proper seat and harness can help support your body, but keeping your left foot placed against the dead pedal makes a huge difference. If you're left-foot-braking, keep your left foot braced against the dead pedal until it's needed to brake—don't have it hovering over the brake pedal while cornering.
- If your left foot is hovering above the brake pedal, it's possible—even likely—that it'll relax and rest against the brake pedal, even slightly. This creates heat in the brake pads, calipers, and disks (something it usually doesn't need), wears them out faster, triggers the brake lights (so that

following drivers don't know whether you're braking for some reason), and can actually slow you down. In some cars, this can also fool the electronics into believing you actually want to brake, and it'll reduce the throttle.

- Most modern cars are sensitive to any amount of simultaneous overlapping of braking and throttle use. This is a result of the reported cases of unintended acceleration where a driver was supposedly braking and the car still accelerated. For this reason, most cars are designed so that if you apply the brakes, any amount of throttle—and therefore acceleration—is completely cut out.

Imagine left-foot-braking while you make a left turn in an intersection, where you also apply the slightest amount of throttle. Your car's computer will shut down any amount of acceleration until you've completely released the brakes. If another car approaches you while you're making this left turn, you can see the danger of having any overlap between braking and acceleration on many modern cars.

Taking that car to a racetrack, you're going to experience the same thing if you begin to apply any amount of throttle before you've completely released the brake pedal. That won't be what you want.

With all this in mind, what to do? Left-foot- or right-foot-brake? All things being equal (which they rarely are!), here are my recommendations:

- If you drive a car with a clutch, stick to right-foot-braking.
- If you drive a car without a clutch, use left-foot-braking—but only if you're going to have the opportunity to focus on developing your left-foot skills. Realize you're going to have to develop this skill properly, and this is going to take time and effort. Otherwise, you'd be better off right-foot-braking.

You can see that how you use the brakes isn't as simple as you might have thought. In fact, there's one technique or skill that separates the best drivers from the rest: what they do with the brakes. Before you get the wrong impression, this doesn't necessarily mean braking at the very last moment for a corner. I'll discuss this later, but for now I'll plant the seed: it's what you do when you release the brakes that make the biggest difference. It's when you begin to release them, and how gradually you release them, that matters.

CLUTCH

The clutch pedal is the optional one in the bunch. If you have a typical manual transmission car, you know all about the clutch pedal. If you drive an automatic, you may or may not know how to use the clutch—but that doesn't matter if you're driving an automatic. And if you drive a semiautomatic with paddle shifts, you don't need to worry about the clutch, either.

Since the clutch is all about shifting, and that's a big topic on its own, it gets its own chapter.

7 SHIFTING

Is the manual transmission doomed or dead? Or is it alive and well, and going to be around for a long time?

Start with asking yourself how important fun is to your driving experience. Most would agree that shifting engages you in the act of driving, which is more fun. Some would argue that shifting manually is an unnecessary burden, one that distracts you from more important things (like having fun). To each their own. But to the pure high-performance driver, shifting is part of the fun. It's part of connecting the driver with the car.

One thing is certain: when you shift manually, it's harder to tune out and not pay attention to your driving, at least to some extent. That may be a good thing, or it may be a bad thing. I think it's a good thing to pay attention, and to me it's an important part of being a high-performance driver.

If the manual transmission is dead, as some say, then why do so many enthusiasts clamor for the opportunity to drive with one? Why is there a Manual Transmission Preservation Society page on Facebook? Why are some automakers going out of their way to produce (admittedly, at low volume) cars with manual transmissions? Why? To appeal to drivers like you and me.

Some say the manual is impractical now that automatics and semiautomatics are so efficient and effective. The same could be said for high-heel shoes, hunting with a crossbow, or even using stairs in a building with elevators, but that doesn't stop people from wanting them.

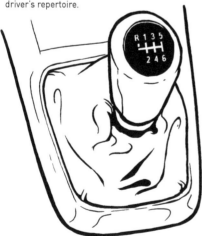

The manual H-shift transmission is still a part of a high-performance driver's repertoire.

Today, fewer than 10 percent of new vehicles sold in the United States are equipped with manual transmissions. The main reason is that the average motorist doesn't want to be engaged in the act of driving—they want to put the least amount of effort into driving.

Another reason is because automatics or semiautomatics are, well . . . better. No driver in the world can shift as consistently or as quickly as a modern automatic. Let's face it: many full-on race cars use dual-clutch automatics for this very reason—they're track proven.

From my perspective, one type of transmission is not better than another. What I will say is that the best high-performance drivers know how to use each of them equally well. In this chapter, therefore, I'll cover all three types of transmissions: fully automatic, paddle-shift/semiautomatic, and manual. We could include constant velocity transmissions (CVTs) here, but there are so few being sold that we'll ignore them—mostly because their operation is essentially the same as driving a fully automatic.

AUTOMATIC TRANSMISSION

Modern automatics, with electronic controls and eight gears, are smooth and efficient. By efficient, I mean that there is little to no slip in them, as was once the case with older automatics. That's also why they perform so well, equal to and often better than manuals.

It used to be that in a full acceleration run (drag race), a manual would always beat an equal car with an automatic transmission, simply because there was a certain amount of slip in the automatic. Not anymore. Thanks to computer controls, different types of "clutches," and additional gears, automatics can keep up with and often beat manuals. The great thing is they're consistent—they don't rely on the skill of the driver to make the difference.

Most automatics have the advantage of learning the driving characteristics of the person behind the wheel, and they'll adapt the timing of shifts based on things like the aggressiveness of the driver. If you drive on the track a lot, run at full throttle often, and look for full acceleration, the computer controlling the transmission will adapt the shift points. And that improves the acceleration rate of the car. If you drive in rush-hour traffic a lot, such a car will adjust shift points to that type of driving.

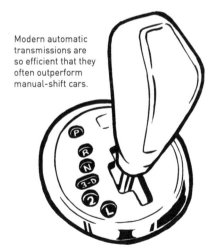

Modern automatic transmissions are so efficient that they often outperform manual-shift cars.

How do you use an automatic for high-performance driving? For many cars, any advantage of manually shifting the automatic is practically nonexistent. In other words, put it in Drive and focus on all the other aspects of driving (covered in this book). Don't bother manually shifting up and down through the gears. The computer-controlled automatic transmission will do as good or better a job of selecting the right gear at the right time than you will.

That depends on the performance level and, often, the price of the car. For example, some higher-priced performance cars will perform as well without manually shifting; a car designed and built to have lower performance and price may benefit from manually shifting, just a little.

Many drivers with automatics spend too much mental and physical energy manually shifting when they should be focused on other things. They think that manually shifting the automatic will improve their performance, but it doesn't.

Some of these drivers are manually shifting for the fun and challenge, and that's not a bad thing. But some think they're improving the performance of their car, when in fact they probably aren't. For others, because their car has an automatic that does not perform well, they are actually helping it get around a track faster. But there are fewer and fewer of these cars on the road and track each year, as automatic transmissions improve, even in lower-priced cars.

If you're shifting your automatic for the fun of it, don't confuse that with looking for more performance. There's nothing wrong with shifting for fun, as long as you're not fooling yourself into believing it makes you faster (unless it truly is).

In most cases, it's best to put your automatic in Drive and focus on driving the right line through the corners, balancing your car's weight, managing the brake and gas pedals, using your vision properly, and so on. That's why automatics are so good: they allow you to focus on everything else.

Many automatic-transmission cars offer different modes. They'll have a basic mode for everyday driving and then provide some kind of "Sport" mode (or modes). These change the shift points (at what rpm rate the engine is allowed to rev before upshifting) and sometimes the throttle response of the engine, resulting in better performance. Some cars come with multiple modes, including "Race," with even more aggressive shifting programs. All of these automatics are controlled by a computer, which allows you to select them on the move.

PADDLE-SHIFT/SEMIAUTOMATIC TRANSMISSION

Paddle-shifting eliminates the need to use the clutch and all that goes along with that. No need to think about heel-and-toe (which I'll cover shortly), no need to manage clutch control—nothing but flicking a lever or button on the steering wheel.

These have the same advantage of a fully automatic: you don't need to worry about what you're doing with your feet. You *do* have to use your hands to select the right gear at the right time (unless you choose to leave it in automatic mode and have the car do that for you).

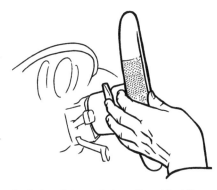

Semiautomatic transmissions with paddle shifters on the steering wheel provide the best of both worlds—the ability to shift while keeping both hands on the steering wheel.

As there is no clutch pedal to operate, your left foot is available as an option for braking.

You will have the option of timing when you shift, up and down, which I'll get to shortly when we discuss manual transmissions. But let's start with one critical message: always complete your downshifts prior to corners, and do as little upshifting in corners as possible.

Why do you want to complete all downshifts before turning into a corner? Anyone who's done this knows the reason: the downshift causes a sudden amount of engine braking effect, which upsets the balance of the car, often resulting in the car beginning to skid or slide.

Some dual-clutch automatics have what is called an "auto blipper" that revs the engine without the driver doing anything as the transmission downshifts. This results in a smooth downshift, something that all great high-performance drivers who drive a manual have learned to do. While this does make it better if you should downshift while cornering, it's still best to always complete your downshifts prior to turning.

SPEED SECRET

Do as little shifting in corners—complete downshifts before, and minimize any upshifts while turning.

MANUAL TRANSMISSION

Even manual transmissions are becoming less manual than they were in the past. Anti-stall, hill-control systems, and auto-rev (a feature in some manuals that applies an "auto blipper," like a dual-clutch transmission that revs the engine while downshifting) make using a manual easier than ever before. Some say these devices and systems take away from the art of driving a manual. We could argue this point all day long, but the fact remains that they're here to stay. Automakers have come up with clever systems to make driving manuals easier, a factor that may actually preserve the manual for many more years to come.

Whether your car is equipped with anti-stall technology or not, getting a manual transmission car underway and moving is one of the bigger challenges facing a driver new to the world of shifting. Add a hill to the equation and things get even more challenging.

If you're just learning to start with a manual transmission, you want to fine-tune your skills, or you're teaching someone else, learn in a deserted parking lot. With your car sitting still in a relatively flat, large parking lot, depress the clutch and place the shifter in first gear. Now, without touching the gas pedal, slowly—and I mean *slowly*—begin releasing the clutch pedal. As it reaches the point where it begins to engage, hold the pedal still—do not let up on it. The car should begin to move just a tiny bit. Ease up on the clutch pedal a little bit more, slowly. The car should move a little more. Keep gently and slowly easing up on the clutch pedal

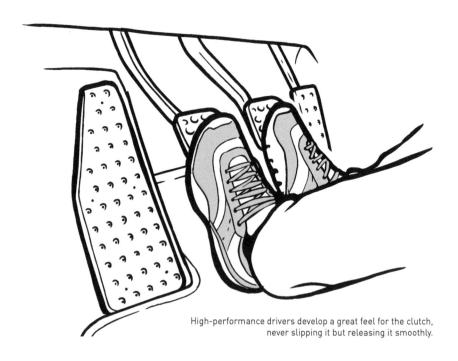

High-performance drivers develop a great feel for the clutch, never slipping it but releasing it smoothly.

until it is fully released, with your left foot moved over to the dead pedal, and the car is moving along in first gear without you touching the gas pedal.

Depress the clutch and come to a stop, and do this over again. And again. And again. You're developing the fine muscle control to manage your clutch pedal by doing this repeatedly. Having this control will make starting on a hill, and every other aspect of shifting easier.

Now that you're moving, let's talk about shifting.

SHIFTING GEARS

Unless your car is equipped with a fully automatic transmission, the decision of when to shift, up and down, is important. It's more than important: it's critical to the overall performance of your car, and to you as a high-performance driver.

Let's start with upshifting. Shifting up to the next tallest gear, from first to second, second to third, and so on, should be done with precision and finesse. If you're driving a manual transmission with an H shift pattern, move the shifter with an open hand instead of grabbing the shift knob: this greatly reduces the chance of missing a gearshift—placing it in the wrong gear, such as from second to first instead of second to third gear.

To minimize the chances of shifting into the wrong gear, move a manual shifter with an open palm, never grasping the shift knob tightly. Shift with finesse.

There is a misconception that high-performance drivers (and race car drivers) shift as fast as possible. Rather, they focus on consistently making every shift as *accurate* as possible. They rarely miss a shift because they're focused on smoothness and precision more than the speed of the shift.

If you're driving a paddle-shift car, missing shifts is nearly impossible, as all you have to do is pull on the appropriate paddle and the car does the rest for you. It's nearly impossible—and not impossible. Pulling on the wrong paddle is possible; building the right programming or habit for operating the appropriate paddle is critical.

There are more than a few situations where it's best to upshift prior to the maximum rpm point. In other words, earlier than you would normally shift up to the higher gear. This is called short-shifting.

When accelerating out of a corner, there are times when it's awkward to upshift. For example, it may be that you're so busy with the steering that it's difficult to remove your hand to work the shifter. Obviously, this is an area where paddle shifts offer an advantage, since you don't have to take your hands off the steering wheel to shift. But even with a paddle shifter, upshifting in the middle of a corner can upset the balance of the car, making it better to shift prior to getting to the corner.

There may be a situation where you want to drive the next corner in a taller gear—let's say fourth gear—but you're not quite at the ideal rpm to upshift before you get there. Instead of holding third gear into the corner, then trying to upshift, you're better off short-shifting into fourth and focusing on driving the corner.

Learn to feel the right rpm rate at which your car should be shifted for its best performance.

There are also times when, because of a downward elevation change, you don't need (or even want, if there's also some cornering going on at the same time) to take the engine to redline before shifting. There are times when it's best to shift before your engine reaches redline to achieve maximum acceleration.

It's these times when you're upshifting before your engine's redline (that is, when you're short-shifting, upshifting prior to your engine reaching its redline), that this technique offers an advantage.

Let's now switch gears and talk about downshifting.

First, why downshift? If you think it's to "slow your car down," you're wrong: that's what the brakes are for. The correct answer is to get the car in the right gear for accelerating after whatever it is you slow down for, such as a corner.

Using the engine to slow the car by downshifting is a common misconception, possibly a leftover technique from decades ago. Think about it: downshifting to slow the car only uses the driving wheels, typically two. You have brakes on all four wheels, so use *them* to slow the car.

This misconception about downshifting comes from the days when cars had very weak brakes, and a driver needed to use the engine to help slow the car. With a couple of very rare exceptions, any car manufactured within the past few decades has brakes that are more powerful than the engine. Use the brakes to slow the car,

SPEED SECRET

When approaching a corner, use the brakes to slow the car, not the engine by downshifting.

and only downshift to get into the best gear for accelerating out of the corners. This means slowing the car with the brakes, wait, and then downshift. The key is to slow the car enough *before* downshifting. Hold off on

SPEED SECRET

Heading towards a corner, brake . . . wait . . . then downshift.

downshifting as much as possible, while still being able to complete it before turning into the corner (with your left foot off the clutch pedal and braced against the dead pedal).

If you're driving a manual shift car, one of the techniques that you may have heard of is "heel-and-toe" downshifting. Anyone who drives a manual transmission car should use this technique when downshifting. It does take practice to become proficient, but so does every other performance-driving technique. It's worth it. Why? Because it's easier on your transmission and engine, helps keep your car better balanced, makes braking more effective, and provides you with more control. Plus, what you do with your feet when heel-and-toeing and the revving of the engine also makes you look and sound good! And every driver worth their weight in feathers, and better, uses it.

See below for the how-to of heel-and-toe. But for now, let's talk about why you would use the heel-and-toe technique.

Let's say you're driving along in fourth gear and you downshift to second gear for a corner. As you let the clutch out when completing the downshift, the additional engine braking effect causes the car to jerk or lunge. There's a sudden, extra amount of deceleration, which results in a jerky movement. That upsets the balance of the car. It also puts an extra amount of braking force on the driving wheels (the ones the engine drives through: front tires on a front-wheel-drive car, rear tires on a rear-wheel-drive car, all tires on an all-wheel-drive car). This can cause those tires to begin to skid if you're traveling fast enough (or the road or track surface is even slightly slippery) to be at or near the tires' traction limit. That is one major reason to always have your downshift completed before you turn into a corner. If you let the clutch out while cornering, it can cause or exacerbate the skid.

Follow this rule: don't turn the steering wheel into a corner until you've completely released the clutch pedal and placed your left foot on the dead pedal again. Keep your left foot there until you absolutely must depress the clutch— don't hover over the clutch pedal.

If you're driving a paddle-shift car, complete your downshift before turning into the corner.

Another reason for completing your downshift before the corner is that your body needs the support of your left foot on the dead pedal. Place it there and

SPEED SECRET
There are no downsides to a smooth downshift!

brace your body with it. Try it, then make it a habit to have it there every second you're not using the clutch.

You may also know that it's smoother if you give the throttle a quick "blip," revving the engine just before letting the clutch out on a downshift. If done correctly—with the right timing and the right amount of engine revving—you won't feel the downshift at all. That's a good thing. That should be your goal with each and every downshift. The smoother your downshift, the more control you have of your car, and the less wear and tear on it.

So if your left foot is depressing the clutch and your right foot is blipping the throttle, what's doing the braking? After all, the reason you're downshifting is to be in the best gear for accelerating away from a slower speed.

This is where heel-and-toe comes in. With this technique, you use your right foot to brake and blip the throttle at the same time. Tricky stuff? It can be. In fact, it will be challenging until you've developed a mental program, a habit, for doing it. Eventually, it will become as natural as turning the steering clockwise to make a right turn: you won't think about it, you'll just do it. That takes practice.

HOW TO HEEL-AND-TOE DOWNSHIFT

Here is a step-by-step explanation of how to heel-and-toe downshift:

1. Begin braking, squeezing the brake pedal with the ball of your right foot (having pivoted your right foot, with heel on the floor, from the throttle).
2. Get your left foot in position to depress the clutch—but not yet. Continue braking, increasing pressure to maximum braking effort.
3. Depress the clutch pedal.
4. Move the shift lever into the next lower gear.
5. Continuing braking and, with the clutch still depressed, pivot your right foot at the ankle and let the right side squeeze the gas pedal, blipping the throttle (that is, revving the engine).
6. Still maintaining your braking, ease the clutch out. Place your left foot back on the dead pedal.

A common error drivers make is to depress the clutch (3 above), blip the throttle (5), move the shifter into the next lower gear (4), and then let

SPEED SECRET
Shift—blip—release clutch.

the clutch out (6). Notice that blipping the throttle and moving the shifter are in the wrong order. The problem is that, by the time they've moved the shifter and begun letting the clutch out, the engine's revs have already started falling, and it's almost as if the driver hadn't blipped the throttle at all.

Instead, be sure to depress the clutch (3), move the shifter (4), blip the throttle (5), and quickly follow that by releasing the clutch (6). Think *Shift— blip—release the clutch*.

If possible, keep the heel of your right foot on the floor at all times. By doing this, you have a better pivot point for your foot, and you're using the small muscles of your foot and ankle, rather than the bigger ones in your calf and thigh. You have better, more finely tuned movements with these smaller muscles than you do the bigger muscles in your leg, and you'll have more accurate control of the brake pedal and blip of the throttle.

Not all cars allow you to keep your heel on the floor, or the ability to rock

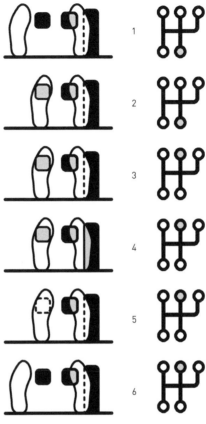

Illustrated here are the steps for heel-and-toe downshifting.

and pivot your foot to blip the throttle with the right side of the bottom of your right foot. In some cars, you need to adapt and compromise. But start by trying to keep your heel on the floor and pivoting your foot at the ankle.

Notice that the term "heel-and-toe" is a bit misleading. Once, decades ago, a driver would actually apply the brakes with his heel and blip the throttle with his toe, which is the origin of the term. Since the pedals have been moved closer together, the term should actually be called "ball-of-foot-and-side-of-foot."

Braking is your top priority throughout heel-and-toe downshifting. Never sacrifice braking for anything else. While there is no wrong way of moving your right foot to brake and blip the throttle at the same time, there is one thing you should avoid if possible: applying the brakes with anything other than the ball of your foot. For example, pressing on the brake pedal with your heel is not nearly as good as using the ball of your foot. Your heel doesn't have the sensitivity, and in such a movement you no longer have your heel on the floor.

As you pivot or rock your foot to blip the throttle, it's important to keep consistent pressure on the brake pedal. It's actually pretty easy to allow the movement of your foot to ease up, then down on the brake pedal while blipping the throttle. That's a no-no: you should keep consistent pressure on the brakes while blipping the throttle, and that simply takes practice.

Speaking of practice, heel-and-toe is all about practice. At first it may seem nearly impossible to get the timing just right and put all of the pieces together. Soon, though, you'll find that you're able to do it—if you practice it enough. Then, you may find yourself driving a different car, with the pedals in different positions, and the responsiveness of the engine when you're blipping the throttle will also be different. It may seem like you're going back to the beginning and learning the process all over again. You should be able to adapt to the car and become proficient at the technique, as you were before. When you move to another car, you'll have to learn that one, then another, then another, and so on. Eventually, you'll be able to adapt to any car within a short period of time. It isn't impossible, but it takes practice.

I recommend that you learn and practice heel-and-toe on the street before using it for the first time on the track. Having said that, I strongly recommend *not* practicing it in traffic. Instead, find a deserted piece of road, accelerate up to top gear, brake and heel-and-toe downshift all the way down to second gear, then accelerate back up to top gear and do it all over again. Keep doing this until you're able to do it consistently, smoothly. Once you're comfortable with the technique and timing, even if you're not perfectly smooth, begin using it with each and every downshift when driving on the street. Make it part of your mental programming—a habit. Eventually, you'll get to the point where it's almost as if you can't *not* do it.

When you drive on a track, heel-and-toe downshifting will actually seem easier. Why? Because when you're driving on the track, you brake harder than you do on the street. And when you brake harder, the pedal becomes more firm, making the pivoting of your foot to blip the throttle easier to control.

Remember that heel-and-toe downshifting allows you to brake and blip the throttle at the same time, so your downshift becomes smoother, causing less wear and tear on your car and allowing you to maintain better control over your car.

SKIP-SHIFTING

Imagine you're approaching a corner. If you have to downshift from, say, fourth to second gear, there are two ways you can do it:

- You can downshift from fourth to third, and then from third to second.
- You can downshift directly from fourth to second, without going through third.

The second method is called skip-shifting, because you skip going through the intermediate gear(s).

The benefit of skip-shifting is that you're doing less. Anytime you do less, that's less opportunity for an error, and it can help make your driving smoother. The downside of skip-shifting is that it's harder to get the timing just right so that you don't either over-rev the engine or over-slow your car.

I don't recommend starting with skip-shifting, but once you become proficient at consistently smooth downshifts, it's something that I suggest. It's not for all cars and drivers, but the more you do with the controls, the more opportunity you have for making an error. Minimize what you do by skipping gears when downshifting.

Finally, where possible, use one gear higher or taller (use third gear rather than second, for example) than you think you need for any particular corner. Too many drivers feel that they need to be busy, shifting up and down the gears, revving the engine, and generally making more work for themselves than necessary. Shift as little as possible. That way, you can focus on more important things (we'll get to those more important things later), and you'll be less busy (that's a good thing).

SPEED SECRET

The less you do with the controls, the fewer errors you'll make, and the smoother and faster you'll drive.

VEHICLE DYNAMICS

"Vehicle dynamics" is a fancy phrase for what your car does when it's in motion.

There are only three things you can do with your car: brake, corner, or accelerate. Whenever you do one or some combination of those things, you decelerate, change direction, or accelerate the car. But something else happens, too. You cause a transfer of the vehicle's weight.

TIRE TRACTION AND WEIGHT TRANSFER

Before I elaborate on causing weight to transfer, think about this: there are only four things that connect your car to the road or track surface:

High-performance drivers understand that it's their tires that make the difference—the four tires of a car are what connect the driver to the road.

1. Tire
2. Tire
3. Tire
4. Tire

Yes, you have just four tires in contact with that surface, gripping that surface. And, there's only a small part of that tire in contact with the road or track at any time. That part of the tire is called the "contact patch."

Go look at a tire on your car. Did you notice that just a small percentage of the entire tire is actually touching the

At any moment in time, there is just a small amount of the tire in contact with the road surface (the tire contact patch).

SPEED SECRET

The better your understanding of your tires, the better you'll be as a high-performance driver.

ground? In fact, it's not that much bigger than your outstretched hand, and you only have four areas that size connecting your car to the ground. And if it weren't for gravity, they wouldn't even be touching.

Obviously, if you have a wider tire, it will usually have a larger contact patch. But if you were to push down on your tire, putting more weight on it, its contact patch would grow larger, too. Think of pushing a balloon against a table surface—the more you push on it, the larger the balloon's area that would be touching the

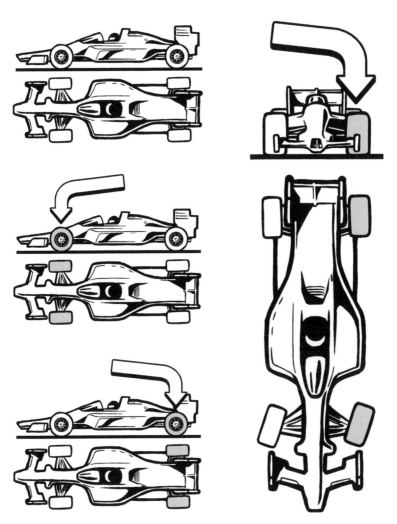

Weight is transferred when a car accelerates, brakes, or corners. As weight transfers onto a pair of tires, the tires on the opposite side or end of the car become less weighted.

table. Generally, the larger the contact patch, the more grip or traction the tire has with the track surface.

Think about your car when it's sitting at rest or when it's moving at a constant speed in a straight line. The weight of the vehicle is distributed relatively equally over each of the four tires. Let's say you have a car that weighs 2,000 pounds; each tire has 500 pounds pushing down on it. In reality, every vehicle isn't perfectly balanced, so the front or rear tires are going to carry a little more of the weight than the others. Even the weight from side to side is rarely perfectly balanced, but it's close. And because it's close enough, we'll assume that it's equal in our example.

If you were lying under a glass road, you'd be able to look up at each tire's contact patch, either as the car was sitting still or as it traveled down the road. In our example, each of the tire contact patches is the same size and shape, as each has an equal amount of weight on it.

As you know, when you brake, the front of the car dives down. When that happens, weight has transferred forward, putting more weight on the front tires, taking some off the rears. In our 2,000-pound car example, you might now have 600 pounds on each of the front tires and 400 on each of the rears. Notice that the total stays the same (600 + 600 + 400 + 400 = 2,000), only the distribution of weight has changed. If you were observing from below, the contact patches of the front tires also got larger, while those of the rears got smaller.

When you accelerate, weight shifts to the rear and the back of the car squats down. The rear tires now have more weight on them than the fronts. In this case, the contact patches of the rear tires grow, and the fronts shrink.

Note that this doesn't change whether you're driving a rear-wheel-drive, front-wheel-drive, or all-wheel-drive car. The laws of physics don't care which tires are driving your car forward: weight transfer happens, no matter what type of car you're driving.

For this reason, all cars have larger brakes on the front, because the front tires do more of the braking, due to the forward weight transfer. Similarly, most

Any tire with more weight on it has a larger contact patch and generates more grip or traction.

purpose-built race cars (Top Fuel drag and Formula One cars, for example) are rear-wheel-drive and have larger rear tires, because the rear tires have more traction when accelerating.

When you go around a corner, weight transfers to the outside tires, and the contact patches of those tires get bigger. For example, when you go around a right-hand corner, the car's weight is transferred onto the left-side tires, and weight is taken off of the right-side tires (the inside tires' contact patches get smaller). If you think about holding a hot cup of coffee between your legs while driving (not recommended!), which leg gets burnt when it spills from going quickly around a right-hand corner? Your left leg. That's because weight of the liquid is transferred to the outside, so that it slops out of the cup.

When weight is transferred onto a tire it gains traction, so the contact patch gets bigger. Think of moving a rubber eraser along a piece of paper: if you're pushing lightly down on it, it's easy to slide; but if you push down hard on it, it takes more effort to move it along the paper. The same is true with the tires on your car—with more weight on them, they have more traction or grip.

Remember, though, that as weight is transferred to one end or side of the car, the opposite end or side loses weight, and therefore those tires lose grip.

Here's the really interesting thing: *the tires that gain grip do not gain as much as the opposite tires lose.* This means that, though the total amount of weight hasn't changed, the total amount of available grip or traction from the tires *has* changed. This has to do with the way rubber tires interact with the road or track surface; the fact that, with more weight, the tires have to do more work; and a bunch of other technical stuff that we, as drivers, don't really need to understand.

What we do need to know—at a very deep-down-inside, know-it-inside-and-out level—is that, when we cause weight transfer, we have less overall traction to work with. That may seem unfair, but that's physics for you.

TRACTION UNIT NUMBER

I use something I call the traction unit number model to explain this.

With your car moving at a constant speed in a straight line, its weight is distributed equally over all four tires. If we took a "traction-o-meter" and measured how much traction each tire had, they would return an equal amount.

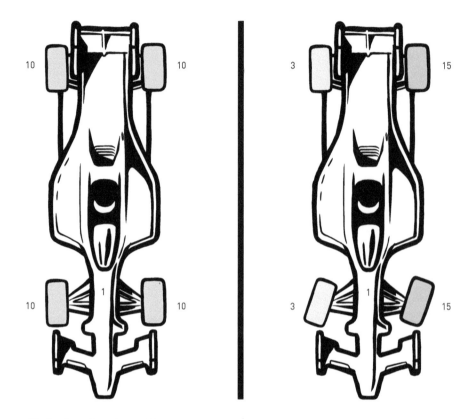

The traction unit number model.

Let's say that each tire has ten units of traction. If you add them up, you have a total of forty units holding your car on the road or track surface.

When you go around a corner, weight transfers onto the outside tires, increasing their traction. In our model, they will now have fifteen units of traction each. But, as I said, the tires on the inside are now unloaded, losing some of their traction. And because they lose more than the outside tire's gain, they now have three units of traction each. When you add that up (15 + 15 + 3 + 3), you now have a total of 36 units of traction holding your car on the road or track.

This is only a conceptual model, and there is no such thing as a "traction-o-meter." Don't go into your local tire store and ask for tires with eleven units of traction (unless the store is called Spinal Tap Tires!). Our model can help you understand traction and weight transfer, so that you can learn to manage it better. It's accurate, but the way of measuring a tire's actual traction as it rolls down the road or track is unavailable (at least to the average high-performance driver).

Of course, you can't drive a car without causing some weight transfer. Every time you accelerate, brake, or go around a corner, weight transfer happens. As I often say, that's physics for you. It means that, just when you need it most—like going around a corner—you actually have less traction.

What can you do about this? Cause as little weight transfer as possible. How? By driving smoothly.

Here's an example. You come to a corner, and you're not looking very far in front of you. You abruptly jerk the steering wheel to head into the corner, then realize that you're not quite on the right path. You make an adjustment to the steering, then another to bring it back to the original path. Since you haven't planned ahead, you have to adjust your speed, too. Those steering and throttle adjustments cause some weight transfer, resulting in reduced traction.

Take the same scenario, but this time you're looking way ahead and you've planned out your path and speed through the corner. Your steering input is smooth and consistent, and your acceleration is progressive and smooth. Of course, weight transfer will occur, but not as much. By causing less weight transfer, your car will have more overall traction to work with through the corner.

It's ironic that, when you need it most—when you've not done something right and caused more weight transfer—you wind up with less traction. When you do things right, you have more traction. I guess that's your payoff for doing things right!

SMOOTH IS FAST

This is why smooth is fast. The smoother you drive, the less weight transfer you cause, and the more overall traction you have to work with. The more traction you have, the faster you can drive.

All this to say that you'll be able to drive faster if you reduce weight transfer. One way to reduce weight transfer is to drive very slowly—but this defeats the purpose of putting a car through its paces, on the track, at least. That's why high-performance driving is tricky!

You can counteract this effect if you combine smoothness with speed, which should give you the best of both worlds. This takes deliberate practice, and, again, it's a loop: smoothness leads to more speed, speed leads to more weight transfer, more weight transfer leads to less traction, less traction leads to less speed. But if you can break that pattern somewhat by managing weight transfer, you can use smoothness and changing traction abilities to your advantage.

SPEED SECRET

Smooth is fast.

WEIGHT MANAGEMENT

High-performance drivers are weight managers. You can add or take away weight from any one of your tires through the way you use the brakes, steering wheel, and throttle. Properly applied, you can manage weight transfer to your advantage.

There are times when you want your front tires to have more traction than the rears, such as when you're initiating a turn into a corner. With the rear tires driving your car forward in a straight line, when you turn the steering wheel, you're asking the front tires to overwhelm the rears and change the direction of the car. If the front and rear tires have the same amount of traction, that's a battle that you might win . . . or maybe not. In other words, your front tires may not have enough traction to outdo the rears to the degree that your car will change direction as much as you want.

If you transfer weight onto the front tires, though, they'll have more traction than the rears. This will improve your chances of changing the car's direction and going where you want to go.

A car in motion is constantly transferring weight, and the better you can keep it balanced—by driving smoothly—the more traction it will have.

To transfer weight onto the front tires, you could either brake or simply lift off the gas pedal, right? Lifting off the throttle is a form of deceleration, and deceleration transfers weight forward, onto the front tires and off the rear tires.

To demonstrate the good and bad of weight transfer, what would happen if you were accelerating as you turned into a corner? When you accelerate, you transfer weight onto the rear tires and off the fronts, so it might be difficult to get the car to change direction.

This should give you an idea of the correct technique as you approach a corner, at least from a weight transfer management perspective. We'll return to this later, but it's important that you see the importance of weight transfer.

SLIP AND SLIP ANGLE

If the concept of an unweighted tire losing more traction than a weighted one gains challenged your common sense, here's another one to keep you thinking for a while: a tire has the most traction when it's sliding or slipping a little bit. Again, due to the way the tire interacts with the track surface, it actually has more grip or traction when it's sliding. For most tires, it's when they're sliding by about 3 to 10 percent.

If you think about this percentage of slip when you're braking, the tire would be turning about 3 to 10 percent slower than the car is moving. Let's say your car is traveling 100 miles per hour and, with 3 to 10 percent slip, the tires are rotating at between 90 and 97 miles per hour.

When tires slip this much, they're at the threshold of maximum traction. The term "threshold braking" refers to the point where the tires are on this threshold or edge; if you were to add a tiny bit more pressure on the brake, they would lock up and skid. Of course, if your car is equipped with ABS (Anti-lock Braking System), the computer is keeping the tires at this threshold.

When accelerating with the tires at their very limit, they're turning about 3 to 10 percent faster than the car is moving. By comparison, if you have 100 percent slippage, it would be the equivalent of sitting still with the tires spinning while stuck in snow.

When you're turning, this slip is measured in a different way. In this case, we look at the tires' slip angle.

Imagine steering the front tires into a left turn. If you're at a speed that's near the tires' traction limit, the car won't go exactly where the front tires are pointed. In fact, there will be a certain amount of slip. The difference between the direction the front tires are pointing and the direction the car is moving is the slip angle.

If you measure and graph a tire's slip angle versus its traction, you'll see that the peak traction is when there is a certain amount of slip angle. How much slip depends on the tire, as every type of tire has different slip-versus-traction characteristics.

The graph below tells you two important things:

- If the tires are not slipping a certain amount, they're not at their peak traction.
- Once a tire begins to slip a little bit, that doesn't mean you've lost control of the car. In fact, notice that the traction gradually tapers off with increasing slip.

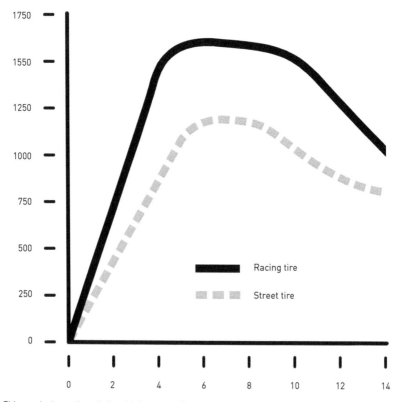

This graph shows the relationship between slip angle and traction.

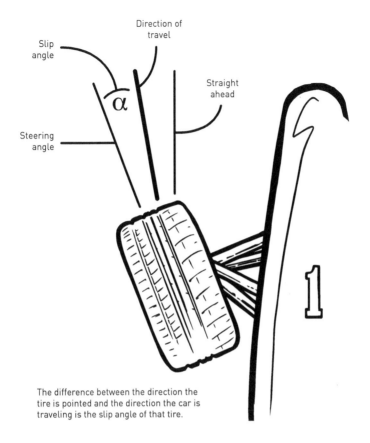

Slip angle

Direction of travel

Straight ahead

Steering angle

α

1

The difference between the direction the tire is pointed and the direction the car is traveling is the slip angle of that tire.

Driving a car at the limit is driving with the tires at their peak slip angle. If a tire generates its maximum traction with 5 degrees of slip, and you're driving with them at 3 degrees of slip, you're not driving at the limit. If you're driving with the tires at 7 degrees of slip, you're driving beyond the limit.

Notice that driving at 7 degrees of slip does not necessarily mean you're going to slide off the road or track and crash—it may be possible to drive at that slip angle all day long without going too far and spinning out, but you won't go as fast as you could with that much slip. In this case, you'll be overdriving the tires.

UNDERSTEERING AND OVERSTEERING

Understeer and oversteer describe the handling characteristics of a car as it travels through a corner. I suspect you've experienced both of them at some point when driving, and you may have even learned a little about controlling them, especially if you've spent time driving on a skid pad or a snow-covered parking lot.

Understeer occurs when your front tires have less traction than the rear tires do: the car tends to push or plow straight ahead (or at least not on as tight a radius through the corner as you'd like). Think of it as the car not turning, or steering, as much as you'd like; for this reason, it's called understeering.

Another way of looking at understeer is that the front tires have a larger slip angle than the rears do. For example, they may have 7 degrees of slip, whereas the rears have 4 degrees: the front tires are sliding or slipping more than the rears.

Oversteer is the opposite: it occurs when the rear tires have less traction than the fronts, and the car tends to follow an arc that is tighter in radius than you'd like. It's also called "loose" or "fishtailing." When the car is turning, or steering, more than you want, it's called oversteering. At its extreme, oversteer leads to the car spinning out.

With both of these handling characteristics, it's what the car is doing, not what you, the driver, are doing. In other words, oversteering is not when you've steered the car too much, and understeer is not when you've steered too little.

What causes these handling characteristics? First, either can be caused by how the car is set up to handle and/or what you do to the car.

Some cars are designed to understeer when they approach their limits. Most street cars are designed to do this for the simple reason that controlling understeer is a little easier. At least, the first reaction that a driver has to an understeering car is more natural, which is why most manufacturers build their cars to understeer: it's easier for an untrained driver to survive this situation.

Your car's natural tendency towards one handling characteristic—either understeer or oversteer—is a result of a number of design factors, such as:

- Engine position in the car, which reflects the static weight balance of the car; a rear-engine car will typically have a larger percentage of the weight over the rear tires, whereas a front-engine/front-wheel-drive car will have more weight over the front tires
- Which wheels are driven (front-wheel drive, rear-wheel drive, all-wheel drive)
- Suspension design/geometry
- Center of gravity of the car
- Tires
- Differentials, torque vectoring, and corner braking systems
- Aerodynamics (both passive and active systems)

Some of these factors can be "tuned," such as suspension alignment, tire sizes, and even pressures, but for most of this book I assume you're driving what you have; this book is not about how to adjust the handling of your car.

As the driver, you also influence how your car handles. In fact, you typically have a bigger impact on your car's handling than its design.

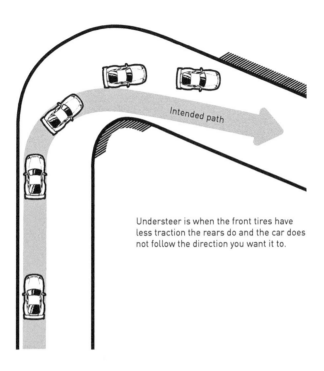

Understeer is when the front tires have less traction the rears do and the car does not follow the direction you want it to.

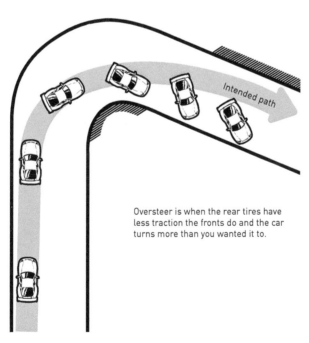

Oversteer is when the rear tires have less traction the fronts do and the car turns more than you wanted it to.

The factors that you control are speed, weight transfer, and what you do with the controls (steering wheel and brake and gas pedals). These influence the handling of your car more than anything.

The first thing to remind yourself is that speed plays a major role. If you drive slow enough, your car will exhibit neither understeer or oversteer—it will pretty much track in a neutral fashion through any corner. But who wants to drive that slow?

If you're driving through a corner and your car begins to understeer, what do you do? Remember that the front tires have less traction than the rears with understeer, so your first goal is to give them more traction. How do you do that? You could brake to transfer weight to the front tires, but the fronts are already lacking traction, so asking them to also brake will likely overload them and make the problem worse.

Instead, if you lift your foot off the throttle, you also transfer weight forward, giving the front tires more traction. This is the priority when controlling understeer, which is why automakers build their vehicles to understeer when approaching the limit. It's the moment of "Oh my, the car isn't turning as much as I want, and if it doesn't starting turning soon, I'm going to slide off the road and crash!" In this situation, your natural reaction is to lift your foot off the gas. That's instinct kicking in—the instinct to curl up in a fetal position and pull your foot up and off the throttle. That's a good thing, because you'll transfer weight onto the front tires as well as slow down. All good, so far.

What is not natural is this: as the car widens its radius and you plow or push more straight ahead than you want, your instinct will be to turn the steering wheel more. While it might be natural, this won't help. Your thinking will be, "This much steering isn't getting me to where I want, so I'll turn the steering wheel even more." The problem is that, since the front tires are already at such an angle to the road or track that they can't turn the car, turning them even more and putting them at an even more extreme angle will not help. In fact, it will make things worse, and the tires will slide even more.

Instead, when faced with understeer, straighten the steering wheel just a little bit, to an angle where the front tires can grip the road. This is just a slight adjustment in your steering, a slight reduction in steering angle. Doing this will go against your instincts, so it takes practice. That's why I highly recommend

SPEED SECRET

Control understeer and oversteer with your vision and managing weight transfer.

spending time on a skid pad, so you can practice this over and over again, building the habit of steering properly when dealing with understeer.

To recap how to control understeer:

1. Ease your foot off the throttle to transfer weight onto the front tires, giving them more traction.
2. Slightly straighten the steering wheel, just enough so that the front tires regain grip on the road/track surface.

Let's now take a look at oversteer: remember that your rear tires have less traction than the fronts have in this situation.

Imagine going around a corner, and the back end of your car slides out. You're oversteering. What do you do? Give those rear tires more traction. Now. It's a challenge, because there are two opposite ways of doing this, and the right one is dependent on what caused the oversteer. Yes, there are actually two kinds of oversteer: oversteer and power oversteer.

The first kind of oversteer is simply when the rear tires have less traction than the fronts. This is most often caused by the weight balance or handling characteristics of the car, but speed is also a big factor.

Power oversteer is driver induced: it's caused by the driver applying too much throttle and generating wheelspin, which breaks the traction of the rear tires and causes the car to slide—to oversteer. If you've ever played around in a snow-covered parking lot, pouncing on the gas pedal and kicking the rear of the car out into an oversteer skid or slide, you know what I'm talking about. Oh, and, power oversteer can only occur in a rear-wheel-drive car (or all-wheel drive that is biased towards rear drive).

With power oversteer, simply ease a little off the throttle to give the rear tires back some of their grip. If it's regular oversteer, squeeze on the throttle to cause some weight transfer to the rear, giving the rear tires more grip.

I wish it was simple, with only one solution to handle every case of oversteer, but it's not. You have to decide, in a fraction of a second, whether the oversteer is caused by too much or not enough throttle. That's why practice time on a skid pad is so valuable.

When you ease on more throttle to transfer weight to the rear, remember that speed is one factor that caused the oversteer. In this situation, you don't need more speed, so when I say ease on more throttle, I mean "ease," and not "*stand on the throttle*"! Be smooth and gentle.

There's one other thing that you must do in whatever oversteer situation you face: look and steer where you want to go.

I'm sure you were told when you first learned to drive to always "steer into the skid." That's valuable advice, but it's confusing, and maybe one of the most confusing things we're ever taught in our lives.

If you're going around a right-hand corner and your car begins to oversteer—say, the rear slides out to the (left) side—which way should you turn the steering wheel? "Into the skid" sounds easy, but for many people it's not a natural choice: which direction is that? If you're oversteering in a right-hand corner, it seems you're skidding toward the inside of the corner; that is, to the right. But the rear is sliding out to the left. So do you turn the steering wheel to the right or the left?

Remember from Chapter 3 that our hands follow our eyes. If you look left, you'll steer to the left; look right and you'll steer right. If you're going around a right-hand corner and the car begins to oversteer, just look where you want to go. In this case, you should look to the left of the direction the car is facing. By doing that, you'll steer to the left—or "into the skid."

No matter where your car is pointing, look where you want to go, and you'll naturally steer in that direction. That will result in you steering into the skid.

For some drivers, this is natural; for others, it's not. In fact, what's natural for some is to look at where they might crash. In our example, driving around a right-hand corner with an oversteering car, it's easy to look directly ahead or to the right—the direction you'll spin toward if the oversteer continues. And that's the exact wrong thing to do.

Remind yourself over and over again, until it becomes a habit: look and steer where you want to go.

To recap controlling oversteer:

- Look and steer where you want to go.
- If you have oversteer, ease on the throttle to transfer weight to the rear, giving the rear tires more traction.
- If it's power oversteer, ease off the gas to give the rear tires more traction.

COMBINING FORCES

You can use your tires' traction for braking, cornering, or accelerating. You can even combine them—to some extent. But ask too much of your tires and you'll find yourself sliding, skidding, or spinning (the deadly Ss).

Chapter 10 covers this point in more detail, but for now keep this in mind: if you ask too much from your tires, they will give up their grip and start to slide too much. If you try braking hard while cornering, for example, you're asking too much from your tires. Or if you stand on the throttle while the steering wheel is still turned a lot to corner, you're also asking too much of the tires. In either case, you've exceeded their limits, and your tires are going to slide excessively, possibly resulting in the car spinning and sliding straight off the edge of the track or roadway.

That's enough theory and background for now. All of what I've just covered in this chapter has been in preparation for getting down a twisty highway (or racetrack) quickly and with maximum control. Let's move on to cornering technique, then come back to the more subtle nuances of vehicle dynamics (driving at the limit).

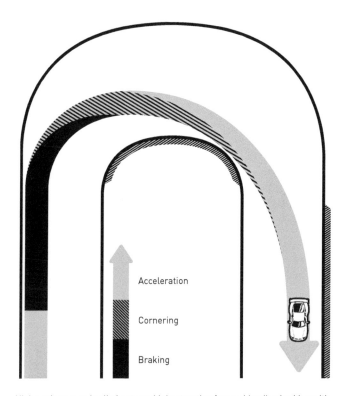

Acceleration

Cornering

Braking

High performance is all about combining traction forces, blending braking with cornering, and then cornering with acceleration.

9 CORNERING

Cornering is the core of high-performance driving. I don't want to take anything away from drivers who drag race, because that takes more skill than most people realize. However, even most drag racers will admit that their form of motorsport is more about the car than the driver, whereas the high-performance driving I'm talking about in this book is more about the driver than the car.

That's not to say that the car's performance isn't important, but a great driver will get more out of a poorly performing car than the other way around.

When you put a corner together, driving along the path you (and the car) want, reaching for the limits, there's something magically satisfying about that. It's when all the pieces come together—your vision, the use of the controls, using the engine and transmission in just the right way, balancing the car to maximize traction, and carving the ideal arc through a turn so you and your car squirt with acceleration out of the turn . . . Well, that's about as good a feeling as anyone can experience.

The concepts and techniques I discuss in this chapter apply equally, whether you're driving on a racetrack, a twisty mountain highway, or the streets heading home from the office. What does change dramatically is the speed and therefore how close you drive your car to its limits. At the same time, whether you're driving at the speed limit or twice that on a track, how you drive the corners is what high-performance driving is all about.

While all of the techniques included in this book can be applied to driving on the street or highway, I recommend practicing all but the basics on a racetrack. Why? The benefits of learning high-performance driving on a racetrack are:

- Traffic is traveling in the same direction.
- Drivers are paying attention.
- It's safer, should you make a mistake—for you and others around you.
- You have more room to experiment with technique.
- You can test the limits of your car more safely.
- Everyone on the track has accepted a certain level of risk.
- Often, a certain technique just doesn't feel completely natural until you're carrying enough speed—speed that is inappropriate for the street.
- It is totally inappropriate and irresponsible to drive near the limits of your car on the road.

The technique that is best practiced on the track is learning how to drive the ideal line through corners. Again, what I share in this chapter applies to driving on the street or highway, but understand that it's easier to grasp the concepts when driving on a track, where the extra speed results in a rhythm that makes everything feel just right. My focus here is on track driving, and I'll trust that you'll apply the concepts to driving on the street and highway—at legal speeds.

THE LINE

Spend more than a few minutes around high-performance drivers, and you'll hear dozens of comments and discussions about "the line." What's all the fuss about?

The line is the pathway that maximizes speed and control on a twisty highway road or racetrack. It's imaginary until you drive it, then it's the direction you drove. Once you get the basic line down pat for a given corner, subtle adjustments can make a significant difference in your speed and control.

The ideal line through a corner is one that results in the least amount of time spent traveling a specific section of road, or the fastest lap time around an entire track—and not just the fastest through that one single corner. There are ways to drive through a corner that will get you through it in less time than from driving a different line, but if it doesn't help what comes after that corner, it often results in a slower overall lap time around the track.

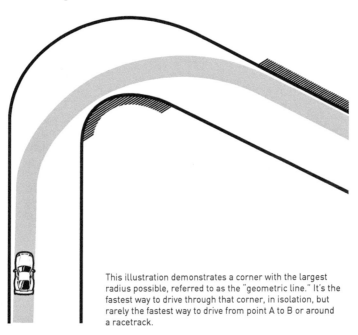

This illustration demonstrates a corner with the largest radius possible, referred to as the "geometric line." It's the fastest way to drive through that corner, in isolation, but rarely the fastest way to drive from point A to B or around a racetrack.

Think about corners and what comes after them. You shouldn't think of them in isolation. Think about driving a line through a corner in such a way that it lowers the overall amount of time spent in that section, or your overall lap time. Sometimes that means you have to give up something early in the corner to gain later in the corner and down the following straightaway.

I'm going to make an assumption here: one of your goals is to get from A to B or around a racetrack as quickly as possible. Sure, control, safety, and consistency are also important, but the one measurable factor is your lap time. While your lap time may not even be the most important factor, we'll focus our discussion in this book on it, for now, because the other factors will fall into place better if you do what's right to minimize your lap time.

This is not to say that your speed is more important than anything else. In fact, smoothness, control, consistency, and safety are all more important. I'm also not saying that if you're fast, all those other things will automatically happen. I mean that, if you drive the line that ultimately leads to a fast lap time around a track, it will partly lead to those other factors.

With that in mind, let's begin our look into the art and science of cornering by identifying some basic concepts or guidelines that apply to cornering.

- Without a doubt, you're going to have to slow down, at least a little, for most corners.
- Whether you're driving on a twisty highway, your local streets, or the track, drive as straight as possible. I know I said that high-performance driving was all about cornering, unlike drag racing, but the straighter you drive, the faster you'll be and the more control you'll have of your car.
- The larger the radius you drive through a corner, the faster you will be (and again, you'll have more control and safety). To prove my point, think about the largest possible radius or arc. It's a straight line, isn't it? Now think about a very tight radius: you'd have to drive much slower through that radius, wouldn't you?
- The larger the radius you drive through a corner, the faster and more in control you can drive. The tighter the radius, the slower you have to drive. If it sounds as though I'm repeating myself, it's for a good reason: this is important stuff.
- Think of driving a twisty highway or racetrack as if it were a series of short drag strips between corners.
- No matter how wiggly a road or racetrack is—and no matter how many corners it has—it's going to have more straightaway (or what is driven as essentially a straightaway) than turns. For that reason, it's more important to maximize your speed down the straightaways than in the turns. What's most important is starting to accelerate early. In fact, the earlier you can begin to accelerate in a corner, the faster you'll be down the straightaways.

- It's not how fast you can go through a corner that matters most. Once again, it's how early in the corner you can begin accelerating that is most important.
- Usually, it's more important to go into a corner relatively slow and come out fast than it is to go into it fast and spend the rest of the corner regaining enough control to allow you to begin accelerating. A message you'll hear over and over again is "slow in, fast out." In other words, you're usually better off going into a corner relatively slow, then coming out of it fast by accelerating early.
- The more references you have to help guide you through a corner, the more consistently fast and in control you'll be.
- As performance drivers, we love the feeling of g-force, and yet the more we can reduce them, the larger the radius we'll be driving (see the third bullet point above).

Let's dig deeper into each of these items. Throughout, keep one thing in mind: each of these concepts or guidelines interrelate and interact with one another, to the point where you may have to compromise one for another.

There are two ultimate goals here:

- Travel from point to point on the street or highway with the most control possible. (If two drivers get from point A to point B in the same amount of time, the driver who does it with the most amount of control—in fact, with control left in reserve to deal with unforeseen situations—is the best driver.)
- Travel from point to point (A to B on a highway; start line to finish line in a lap of a track) in the least amount of time, minimizing your lap time.

REFERENCE POINTS

Let's stop and talk about reference points before moving on, as they really help us define the line we drive through corners.

There are three main reference points in every corner:

- **Turn-in.** This is the point where you initiate your turn into the corner, from the outside edge of the track surface or lane that you're driving in. At this point, you can turn the wheel relatively gently, or rather aggressively—bending into the corners or crisply, as I mentioned back in Chapter 5.
- **Apex.** Think of the apex of a corner as the place where you're no longer entering the corner but transitioning to exiting it. It's the point or area that you clip or hug at the inside of the corner. Notice that it can be exactly in the middle of the corner (the geometric apex), early (early apex), late (late apex), or somewhere in between. Your apex is entirely dependent on where

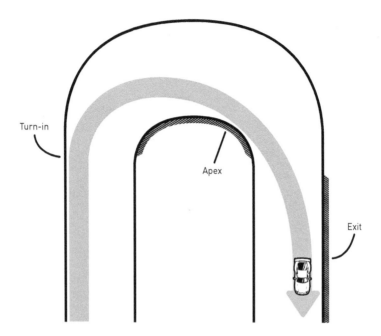

The three most important references you'll use to drive the ideal line through corners are the turn-in, apex, and exit points.

and how you turned into the corner. Typically, it doesn't matter whether you're driving on the street or the track, yet it's always safer to drive using a later apex on the street. The reasons will soon become obvious.

• **Exit.** The exit point is where your car comes out to the outside edge of the lane or track, using up all the surface that is available to you so you can begin accelerating as early as possible (remember, the sooner you unwind, or straighten, the steering, the sooner you can begin accelerating). When driving on the street or highway, you need to stay in your legal lane and save a little cushion for error by staying on the pavement, not using the shoulder of the road.

These are the big three references, the ones that you'll rely on over and over again to help you define and refine the line you drive through all corners. From this moment on in your life, you'll never look at a corner the same way again (if you haven't already been doing this), whether it's a corner on a track or the entry into your driveway at home.

SPEED SECRET

The more references you have and use, the better a driver you'll be.

We'll get into more references, such as where you begin and end braking for a corner and the multitude of other secondary references that give you feedback about whether you're on the right line or not. For now, remember this: the best drivers take in and have more references than lesser drivers. Your takeaway from that statement (referenced in the list of basic guidelines above) is that the more references you can soak up and internalize, the more consistently fast and in control you'll be.

DRIVE STRAIGHT

When do you have the most control over your car, when driving in a straight line or while cornering? Driving in a straight line, right? It's also where you can go the fastest.

What is a straight line? It's an infinitely large radius corner. When I say to drive corners with the largest radius you can, I'm talking about straightening the corner out as much as possible.

Start with your car positioned on the very outside edge of the track surface, or within your legal lane (giving yourself a little margin for error, especially the errors that other drivers make), then drive to the very inside edge of the track or lane, and finally to the outside again. It's this outside-inside-outside approach you want to apply to each and every bend or corner on the road or track, from turn-in to apex to exit.

We're going to call this outside-inside-outside line the "geometric line" through a corner, because it follows the geometrically largest radius. It's the fastest way to get through any single corner in isolation. But this isn't necessarily the fastest way to go from point A to point B, as in getting around a racetrack with the fastest lap time. It's one of those compromises I mentioned earlier. This

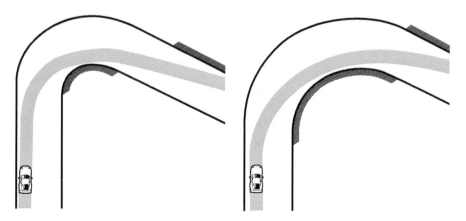

The line you drive through a large-radius corner will be different than one you drive through a tighter-radius corner. Identifying and driving the ideal line through a series of corners is one of the most enjoyable parts of high-performance driving.

The larger the radius you drive, the faster you'll go through that specific corner.

concept—driving in the largest radius possible with an outside-inside-outside approach—is still one of the most important and fundamental guidelines you should keep in mind.

Let's use a racetrack as an example, with the goal of having the shortest lap time (meaning, the fastest going from the start to the finish line, or completing a lap).

If you look at any track, after any corner there's either another corner or a straightaway. The straightaway might be short or long; either way, the faster you get down the straightaways, the faster you'll be all the way around the track. It's been proven over and over—in fact, pretty much from the time auto racing was invented (which was when the second car was built)—that your speed down the straightaways will have more of an impact on your overall lap time than how fast

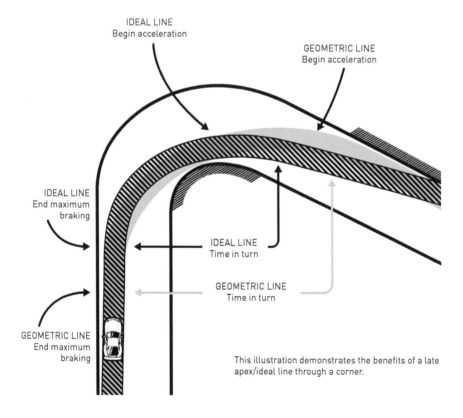

IDEAL LINE
Begin acceleration

GEOMETRIC LINE
Begin acceleration

IDEAL LINE
End maximum
braking

IDEAL LINE
Time in turn

GEOMETRIC LINE
Time in turn

GEOMETRIC LINE
End maximum
braking

This illustration demonstrates the benefits of a late apex/ideal line through a corner.

you can drive through the corners. Of course, your speed through the corners does matter, but mostly in that the speed you carry exiting the corner impacts straightaway speed, which makes the biggest difference.

When I asked you to think about a track as a series of drag strips, connected by corners, this is what I meant. If you use the corners to maximize the speed you're able to carry down the straightaways, you'll have faster lap times. If we were actually racing wheel to wheel (which we're not), you would find it easier to pass other cars on the straightaway than in the middle of the corners. The faster you'd drive down the straightaways, the more likely you could pass on the straights.

How do you use the corners to maximize straightaway speed? I mentioned that there would be some compromising of one basic concept/guideline to benefit another? This is the first place we see this.

Remember that the fastest way to get through a single corner is through the geometric line (the largest radius pathway through the corner). But if you modify this line, you'll be able to start accelerating earlier; accelerate earlier, and you'll be faster down the straightaways. Going faster down the straightaways results in less time spent navigating the entire track (that is, a lower lap time).

Recall from the last chapter about vehicle dynamics that you can only get so much traction out of the four tires on your car. If you're using up all the traction to drive at maximum speed through a corner (one with the largest radius line), you can't begin accelerating until you start to unwind, or straighten the steering—in other words, until you give back some of the traction you're using for cornering to the tires so that they can begin to take on some acceleration. With the geometric line, that means you can't start accelerating until you're pretty much at the outside edge of the track at the end of the corner—the "exit" point.

The only way you can begin accelerating sooner is to begin unwinding or straightening the steering sooner. And the only way to do that is by altering the line you drive through the corner, so that you have an expanding radius in the latter part of the corner. This means you need to drive a tighter radius in the early part of the corner, which, as you know, means that you're going to have to drive slower at that point.

What you're doing is driving a little slower, on a tighter radius, early in the corner to allow for earlier acceleration on a larger—and expanding—radius later in the corner. You're compromising some speed early in the corner for higher speed exiting the corner—and all the way down the following straightaway.

We call this line the "ideal line," since it's ideal for maximizing your speed through—but especially out of—the corner to improve speed on the following straightaway. It results in a lower lap time around a track.

SPEED SECRET

Use corners to maximize your straightaway speed.

The ideal line involves turning in a little later, with a slightly tighter radius, clipping past a later apex while beginning to unwind the steering wheel as you feed in acceleration. (I told you that we'd come back to why a later apex line is preferable.)

The best way to think about this late apex line is that you're going to turn in a little later and sharper, aim for a later apex, then begin accelerating as you unwind (straighten) the steering wheel and head for a later exit point. You can also think of this as making two-thirds of your turning in the first one-third of the corner.

The advantages of this later apex line are as follows:

- It lengthens the straightaway before you have to begin braking for the corner (small advantage).
- It allows you to begin accelerating earlier, because you can begin unwinding (straightening the steering) sooner (big advantage).
- It allows you to see through the corner better, often seeing the exit point before you even turn in.

One disadvantage of the ideal line is that the initial part of the corner has a slightly tighter radius. As I mentioned earlier, a tighter radius means you have to drive slower. That means you'll need to slow down at the beginning of the corner, but you'll also be ready to start accelerating earlier (due to the expanding radius), which easily makes up for the slightly slower corner-entry speed. In fact, there's no doubt you'll be faster at the end of the ensuing straightaway, using the late apex line, than if you drove a geometric line.

COMPROMISES

High-performance driving, and particularly negotiating your way around a racetrack or along a twisty highway road, represents a series of compromises. Often, you must compromise the line and the speed you drive through one corner to maximize your speed in another.

There are times when you also need to compromise the overall amount of traction your car has in order change direction fully enough to get through a corner. At other times, when you'll

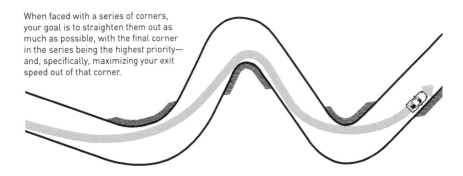

When faced with a series of corners, your goal is to straighten them out as much as possible, with the final corner in the series being the highest priority—and, specifically, maximizing your exit speed out of that corner.

want to use all the grip your car and tires have, you'll need to drive a slightly different line through a corner.

The more you need to rotate a car, as you do in slow or tight corners, the crisper and quicker you should turn the steering wheel. But in long, fast corners, gently arc or bend the steering in. It's not until you put this into practice that the effect really sets in.

With the drivers I coach, I sometimes have them deliberately work on the speed/rate of turning the steering wheel in different corners. It's this deliberate practice that eventually becomes part of the drivers' habits, and they no longer think about it—they just do it.

Racetrack cornering lines are more than just following where someone told you to drive: you have to develop your track driving techniques, adapting how you turn the steering wheel to different layouts of corners.

CORNER PRIORITIES

There's a piece of advice you always hear when show up to drive a racetrack: "the most important corner is the one leading onto the longest straightaway." The thinking behind this advice is strong: you're going to make up more time by being faster on the straights, and the corner that leads onto the longest one gives you the best opportunity to maximize your speed.

The problem with the thinking here is that it's overly simple. Yes, it's not a bad place to start, but the most important corner on any section of road or on a track is usually the fastest one, especially if it leads onto a straightaway of any length.

> **SPEED SECRET**
>
> The slower the corner, the later the apex, and the quicker and crisper you need to turn the steering wheel—and vice versa.

Why? Let me count the reasons:

1. First, the most challenging—in fact, the scariest corners—are almost always the fastest ones. If you're able to master the fastest corner, you're likely to have an advantage over other drivers (if that matters to you). Sure, we're not talking about racing here, but most high-performance drivers want to be faster than other drivers. If you want to gain an advantage over other drivers, you'll probably be able to do that by focusing on and mastering the fastest corners.
2. While you're driving faster through high-speed corners, by the very nature of a larger radius corner, you'll usually spend more time in them. If you're able to carry even 1 mile per hour more all the way through a long corner, it's going to make a huge difference in your lap time around the track.
3. Usually (but not always), slower corners are easier. For this reason, if you begin focusing on getting the fastest corners right from the start, you'll gain an advantage here.
4. Finally, fast corners are less forgiving. I'm not talking about the consequences of spinning off the track in a fast corner (although that's something to consider). Instead, it's important to know what happens if you simply make an error and

When looking at a racetrack, focus on driving the fastest corners that lead onto a straightway first, and then the next fastest, and the next fastest, and so on.

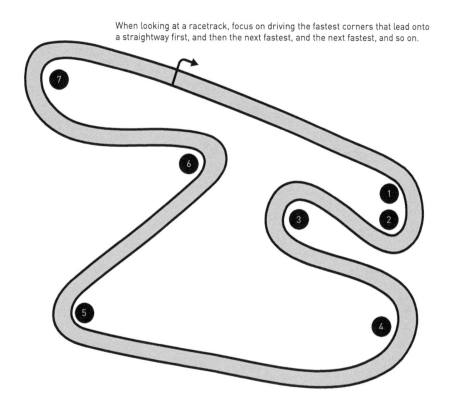

slow too much in a corner. For example, if you're driving through a 40-mile-per-hour second-gear corner, and you make a mistake and slow down

by 2 miles per hour too much, re-accelerating in that low gear is relatively easy. But if you're driving through a fast, 100-mile-per-hour fourth-gear corner, and you over-slow by 2 miles per hour, your car won't accelerate up to speed as quickly.

This doesn't mean that corners leading onto straightaways are unimportant: far from it. They are very important, as any slight advantage you can gain by starting to accelerate early will pay off all the way down the straight. You want to get the corners that lead onto straights right, so that you can begin accelerating early.

When you look at a section of road or a track, though, look at those fast corners first—the ones that lead onto a straightaway, no matter the length. Do everything you can to learn how to drive them well first.

With this in mind, when you look at a track and consider how you're going to focus your time on learning the way to take it at speed, look to the fastest corners first, then the next fastest, and so on. If there's a corner that leads onto a long straight (which there always is), make sure you drive it in a way that maximizes your straightaway speed: focus on getting a strong exit off the corner.

CONTROL PHASES

A good way to think about corners is that they have a number of phases, from the point on the preceding straightaway where you begin braking to the point where your steering wheel is perfectly straight and you're fully accelerating down the following straightaway.

The phases of a corner (shown in the illustration on the next page) are:

1. **Braking.** Apply maximum braking as you approach the corner: think of this as a speed adjustment instead of slowing down (there's a difference, as you'll discover in later chapters).
2. **Trail braking.** As I'll explain in the next chapter, trail braking is where you trail (or ease) the pressure off the brake pedal while turning the steering wheel into a corner, trading off braking for cornering.
3. **Cornering.** This is the area of a corner where you're not braking at all and you haven't begun to accelerate yet. You're using all of the tires' traction for pure cornering.

4. **Transition.** The point at which you transition from braking to acceleration; if you're braking with your right foot, this is where it has released the brakes and is moving over to the gas pedal. If you're left-foot-braking, the transition might be shorter, but it's still there.
5. **Balanced throttle.** Not used in every corner, but, when it is, this means that you've applied just enough throttle to maintain the speed of the car—you're not decelerating (as you would if you weren't applying any throttle)—but you're also not increasing the throttle. This is also referred to as maintenance throttle.
6. **Begin acceleration.** This is the point in a corner where you begin to squeeze on the gas, but you're not at full acceleration yet.
7. **Full acceleration.** By this point, the steering is unwound (straightened) enough for you to return to full throttle.

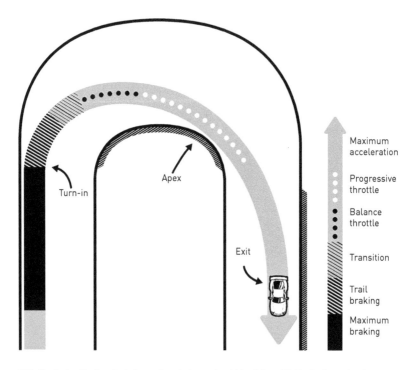

This illustrates the "control phases" —what you should be doing with the brakes, steering wheel, and throttle through a corner.

BRAKE REFERENCES

One of the most important driving techniques, which has led to some of the biggest gains for the most drivers I've trained, is covered in the above Speed Secret.

One day I was driving along a highway in my beater Honda (every penny I had at the time was "invested" in my racing career). Up ahead, the traffic light turned to red. As I started braking, a light bulb lit up over my head.

For a few years, I had wondered why, when other drivers asked me what brake marker I used to start braking for a particular corner, I couldn't tell them. I had

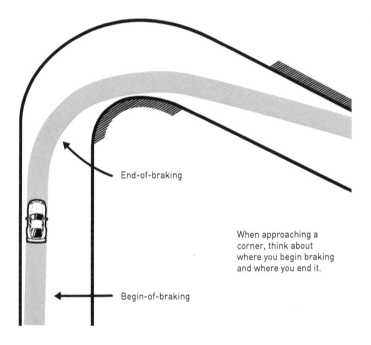

End-of-braking

Begin-of-braking

When approaching a corner, think about where you begin braking and where you end it.

a vague idea, but I couldn't give them an exact answer. I thought there must be something wrong with me for not knowing, but when I realized that I most often outbraked other drivers, I stopped worrying about it.

So, why the light bulb lighting up?

When I braked for the red light, I didn't look around for a brake marker to tell me when to start braking. Instead, I looked ahead to where I wanted to *finish* braking, then began to adjust the pressure on the pedal to suit my intention.

The next time I was on a track, I realized I did something very similar. I used brake markers to give me a general feeling of where to start braking, but what I focused on the most was where I was going to finish my braking—what I began calling the *end-of-braking point* (EoB). It was like I was focused on the stop line at the traffic light.

Over the next few years, I asked other drivers where they started braking for certain corners, and I noticed a pattern in how they answered. The best and fastest drivers couldn't tell me exactly where they started braking, but the slower drivers could.

Where were the best drivers looking? What were they mostly focusing on when heading into the turn? The fast ones were focused on the end-of-braking point, whereas the slower drivers were focused on the begin-of-braking point.

This doesn't mean that a driver should *never* look at brake markers or know where they begin braking, but that *most of your focus* should be on the end-of-braking point, rather than the begin-of-braking point.

When you focus on the end-of-braking point, what does it do to your vision? It forces you to look ahead, into the turn—and what happens when you do that? Typically, your entire brake zone becomes more consistent, and you carry more entry speed into the turn (without it affecting exit speed negatively).

The next time you're performance driving, look for the end-of-braking points. Practice looking into the corner, at the place your foot will finally come completely off the brake pedal.

LEARNING THE LINE

Typically, the reason you'll start driving the line that you do around a racetrack is because that's what you'll be told to do. An instructor will tell you to drive a specific pathway around the track, and you'll connect the dots, as most driver education events and track days use orange cones to indicate the turn-in, apex, and exit points of every corner. In fact, you'll be driving from cone to cone to begin with.

Dig a little deeper: it's critical to understand the *why* behind the line that you drive. That understanding will begin during a classroom training session of your driver event, where an instructor will talk about lines, reference points, and how important they are. With any luck, you'll have a great instructor who helps you see the reasoning for driving a line.

You can only realize your true potential as a driver when you understand this, which will help your adaptability to new tracks, new cars, changing conditions, and even the driving style that you'll develop over time.

Everyone learns in different ways, so this book might lead to the insights and understanding of the lines you should drive. For others, it'll be the driver education classroom training, or a video or online training program that'll switch on the light bulb. Still others won't truly get it until they drive it and other lines, comparing how they feel as they experience them.

Many schools, driver education events, car clubs, and track day organizers want you to drive a specific line. This may not be the fastest line, but it's usually a safer line (meaning that it has a larger cushion for error in case you make a mistake). With more experience, you'll get to the point where you can try variations on the specified line. A good rule that many event organizers use is if you can consistently drive the specified line, and then explain *why* you want to drive a different line, you're ready to do so.

When I say explain why you want to drive a different line, the reason is more than just "it's faster." That's a result, not the *why*. If you can explain why it's faster, then that's getting to a deeper understanding.

"Driving the ideal line" is a huge part of high-performance driving, and it's something that I'm sure you'll incorporate into your everyday driving from now on. You'll look for the ideal turn-in, apex, and exit points, maximizing the radius of every corner, whether on the road or the track.

10 DRIVING AT THE LIMIT

To reinforce what I said in the introduction, driving at the limit means setting whatever limit you choose as your driving goal. To limit your risk, you may make the decision to drive at eight-tenths, or at 80 percent, of your car's potential. That's perfectly okay. All of what I've written in this book still applies. It's just that, rather than driving with the tires at their peak traction level of, say, 5 degrees of slip angle, you may choose to drive at 80 percent of that—at 4 degrees. And let's say your car is capable of generating 1 g of braking, cornering, and acceleration forces (very few cars have the power to accelerate at that level, but it's okay for our purposes to think about it that way); so you've chosen to drive at 0.8 g.

When I talk about driving at the limit, it means the limit the car has, or some limit close to the one at which you've chosen to drive.

THE 100-PERCENT TIRE RULE

You can use 100 percent of a tire's traction for braking. You can use 100 percent for cornering. And you can use 100 percent for acceleration.

But you can't use even 5 percent for accelerating while still using 100 percent for cornering.

You can only ever use 100 percent of your tires' traction, no more. If you want to use 5 percent for accelerating out of a corner, you can still only use 95 percent for cornering. In other words, you'll have to unwind (straighten) the steering wheel by at least 5 percent to use that for accelerating.

You can only ever use 100 percent of your tires' traction, and that's your goal (if you want to drive at the very limit).

Approaching a corner, you can brake using 100 percent of the tires' traction for slowing the car. As you begin to turn the steering wheel, you need to take pressure off the brake pedal—as you use 10 percent for cornering, you'll use 90 for braking; 25 for cornering, 75 for braking; 50 for each; 75 for cornering, 25 for braking. Eventually, you'll use 100 percent for cornering and zero for braking.

> ### SPEED SECRET
> You can only ever get 100 percent out of your tires, but that can be used for a combination of traction forces.

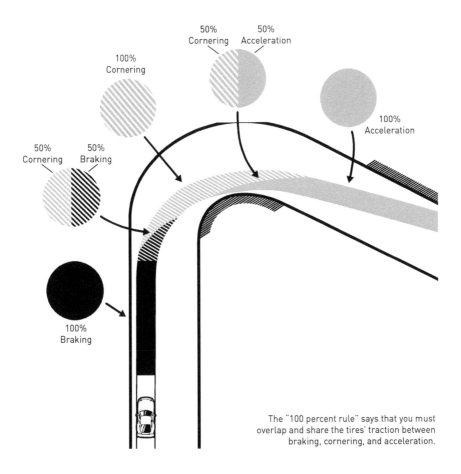

50% Cornering
50% Acceleration

100% Cornering

100% Acceleration

50% Cornering
50% Braking

100% Braking

The "100 percent rule" says that you must overlap and share the tires' traction between braking, cornering, and acceleration.

After cornering at 100 percent, you'll want to accelerate, which means reducing cornering: as you apply the throttle, you'll need to unwind the steering wheel. That equates to 75 for cornering, 25 for acceleration; 50 for each; 25 for cornering, 75 for acceleration; finally, you'll use 100 percent for acceleration on the straightaway.

In reality, you'll often get to full-throttle acceleration before you have the steering wheel perfectly straight, since your car rarely has enough power to exceed or get anywhere near to 100 percent under acceleration. But if you've ever induced power oversteer by tromping on the throttle while turning, especially on a slippery surface, you know what I mean about using more than 100 percent.

This is such a common mistake that there's a term for it: "pinching" the car at the exit of a corner, the act of not unwinding the steering wheel as much or as soon as you should. It's not using all of the track or lane available to you.

To avoid pinching the car, focus on unwinding the steering wheel as early and as quickly as possible while you feed in the throttle.

Imagine that you have a string attached to the bottom of your steering wheel, with the other end attached to the top of the gas pedal when it's fully depressed to the floor. The string is tight. As you turn the steering wheel, the string pulls the top of the gas pedal upward. Once it's pulled all the way up—that is, at zero throttle—the steering wheel will be fully turned to use up all of the tires' traction. Then, as you come out of a corner, you squeeze on the gas pedal and that straightens the steering wheel.

It's this interplay of the throttle and steering wheel that is critical for exiting a corner. Step on the throttle too soon, while you've got too much steering angle still in, and you're asking for more than 100 percent from the tires. That will get you into a skid, slide, or spin.

TRACTION CIRCLE

The traction circle is a graphical way of representing the 100 percent tire rule, as well as describing the limits at which you're driving.

For the moment, imagine that you have a weight hanging from a string from your rearview mirror. When you brake, that weight will swing forward. When you accelerate, it'll swing to the rear. And when you go around a corner, it'll swing to the outside (to the left when going around a right-hand corner; to the right when going around a left-hand corner).

The ultimate amount of grip or traction available from your car and tires determines how far the weight will swing. With lots of grip, it will swing further than if you have just a little grip (imagine the difference between braking on a dry surface versus a wet or even icy one).

Now imagine having a pen on the bottom of the weight; every time it swings, it draws a line on a piece of paper. As you brake in a straight line, it will draw a line forward, in relationship to the amount of g-force you're able to generate. As you accelerate, it'll draw a line to the rear. As you corner, it'll draw a line to the opposite direction of the corner. Imagine that the paper has an X-Y axis graph: the Y axis represents braking and acceleration, or longitudinal g-force, while the X axis represents cornering, or lateral forces. The paper's center, directly in line with the pen as it hangs straight down, represents where it will point when the car is at rest. This is essentially a traction circle graph.

If we calibrate our weight and pen with this graph of longitudinal and lateral g-force, let's say that we can generate 1 *g* when straight-line braking and when we corner at the maximum limit. We should have the same amount of traction when accelerating, so we should be able to generate the same 1 *g*.

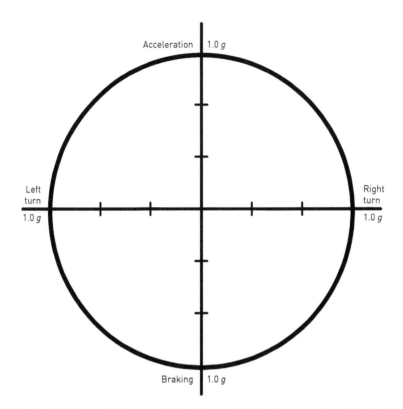

The Traction Circle is a graphical representation of how you blend braking, cornering, and acceleration to use your tires' full capabilities.

If you come up to a corner, brake at the limit (threshold braking or relying on full ABS), let off the brakes, and turn the steering wheel to go through a corner, you won't be using all of the available traction. There will be a small amount of time where the tires will not be at their limit.

Now imagine that you gradually release the brakes while turning the steering as you reach the turn-in point for the corner. This will combine braking and cornering g-force, which draws a circle on your graph. If you keep the tires at their limit—1 g through the corner—you'll keep the pen on the outer edge of a circle. As you begin unwinding the steering wheel, feeding in acceleration, and trading off cornering traction for acceleration, you'll again keep the tires at their limit and continue drawing that circle (as shown in the illustration on the next page).

When you keep the tires at their limit, drawing that circle at the 1-g level on the graph, you're maximizing your speed. That means you're driving at the limit.

In reality, very few cars have enough power to accelerate at the same g-force levels as they can when braking and cornering. This means the line drawn at the

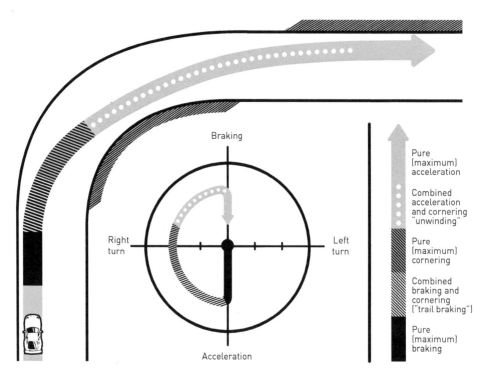

The Traction Circle related to the control phases.

bottom of the graph won't extend quite as far in the other directions: you'll end up with a circle with a somewhat flat bottom.

The traction circle shows you the value of combining braking with cornering, then cornering with acceleration forces, which employs all of the tires' traction.

TRAIL BRAKING

When you gradually ease your foot off the brakes—that is, trail your foot off them—while steering into a corner, we call that trail braking. It's the overlap of braking with cornering, gradually going from 100 percent braking and no cornering, to 75 percent braking and 25 percent cornering, to 50–50, 25–75, and eventually 0 percent braking and 100 percent cornering. (You'll perform this seamlessly, not broken up in steps as I've described here).

Trail braking provides two main benefits:

- First, it keeps some weight transferred onto the front tires, which helps your car turn into the corner.

- Second, the overlap of braking and cornering helps you use all of the tires' capabilities, keeping the tires on the outer edge of the traction circle.

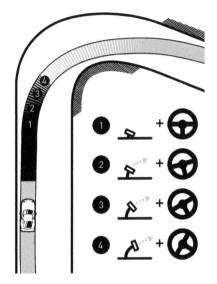

You should also understand what trail braking is not.

It's not necessarily left-foot-braking (yes, you can trail brake with your left foot, but left-foot-braking doesn't necessarily mean you're trail braking).

It's not "braking all the way to the apex." You could brake all the way to the apex, and that would mean you're trail braking, but you could also release the brakes well before the apex—even

Trail braking is the act of easing (trailing) off the brakes as you turn into a corner, trading braking forces for cornering forces.

just a few inches or so past your turn-in point, and that would be trail braking, too.

Some corners and cars reward trail braking, and some don't. As a general rule, the shorter and tighter the corner, the more you should trail brake to help "rotate" the car. The longer and faster the corner, the less you'll want to trail brake.

What do I mean by "rotate the car"? Imagine looking down on your car from above, like from a helicopter. As you turn into a corner, if your car changes direction a lot, it will look as though it's rotating. That's what "rotate the car" means; we can also say that the car "rotated" in the corner. You can think of it as the car oversteering slightly. The variable is that rotating a car is something you do deliberately, and oversteering is not necessarily intentional.

How you rotate the car has a lot to do with how you manage the weight transfer as you turn into a corner, which in turn relates to how you deliberately release the brakes—whether you release them soon and quickly, later and slowly, or some other combination.

SPEED SECRET

How and when you release the brakes will have more effect on how quickly you can drive than where you start braking.

The way your car is set up has an impact on how "willing" your car is to rotate, too. This includes the way the suspension geometry is aligned; the combination of springs, shocks, and anti-roll bars; ride height and rake; and the aerodynamics (especially active aerodynamics on high-end performance cars, such as a moveable rear wing that is activated when braking at high speed).

The *timing and rate of release of the brake pedal* while entering a corner will have a bigger influence on your speed than simply braking later. Of course, that assumes you're already braking close to the limit. In other words, if you're close to braking as late as possible, moving the begin-of-braking later won't improve your lap times as much as getting the brake release *just* right.

Where you begin releasing the pedal in relation to where you start turning into the corner, and the speed at which you release them is the technique used to manage weight to your advantage, while blending the brakes with steering input (cornering) to use all of the tires' traction (100 percent). It's this blending that allows you to carry an extra mile per hour or more into the corner and still get the car to follow the line you want—and to begin accelerating out of the corner as early as possible.

When done just right, it's sort of magical—it keeps the tires at their peak slip angle, you're able to change the direction of the car into the corner with speed, the car generates maximum g-loading, you're managing the weight transfer to balance the car between understeer and oversteer, and you get the car rotated on a path that allows you to start accelerating early, powering out of the corner. Ah, what a feeling!

The deliberate use of the brake release is critical. If I could improve the average high-performance driver's techniques in just one area, it would be their brake release. Many high-performance drivers don't pay enough attention to how they ease off the brakes, and so they miss a critically important part of managing their car. What they typically do is pop their foot off the brake pedal too quickly. Be aware of, and deliberately practice, releasing the brake pedal smoothly.

FAST SWEEPING CORNERS VERSUS SLOW ROTATION TURNS

Not all corners require the same technique when entering them. In fact, it's more likely that every single corner in the world requires a different approach. By that I'm mostly talking about what you do with the brakes as you approach and enter the corner.

SPEED SECRET

In tight, slow corners, use trail braking to help rotate the car; in fast, sweeping corners, reduce the amount you trail brake.

To drive fast, our gut tells us that the later and harder we brake for corners, the better. While that's the case in many situations, it's not correct in all.

I'll use two corners to illustrate my point: a tight, 180-degree hairpin turn that you approach at top speed but have to slow down to 30 miles per hour for, and a long, sweeping corner that you can take at 70. Both corners are approached from a speed of 110 miles per hour. For the slow corner, your speed adjustment before it has you taking 80 miles per hour out of the car. That's a long, heavy braking zone. For the fast sweeper turn, your speed adjustment is only 40 miles per hour.

Because the first corner requires a large change in direction, rotating the car is necessary. It's important to use the timing and rate of release of the brakes—that is, managing weight transfer. If you release the brakes too soon or quickly,

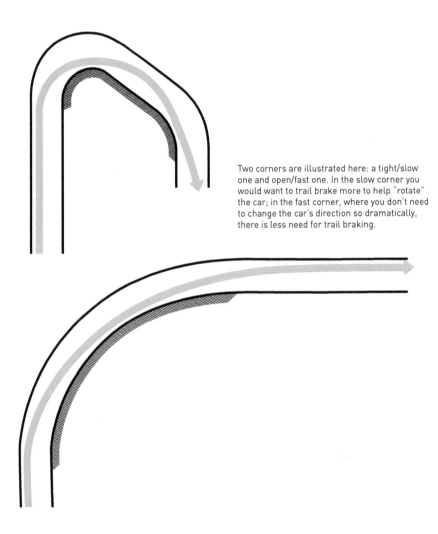

Two corners are illustrated here: a tight/slow one and open/fast one. In the slow corner you would want to trail brake more to help "rotate" the car; in the fast corner, where you don't need to change the car's direction so dramatically, there is less need for trail braking.

the front tires will become unweighted just when you're turning into the corner, causing the car to understeer and not turn as much as you want. But if you release the brakes differently—begin releasing the pedal slightly later, and more slowly—you'll keep the front tires loaded and make it easier to get the car to turn.

This is a typical approach to driving a tight, slow corner. But recall our earlier discussion where we noted that the better balanced a car is (with the least amount of weight transfer), the more overall traction it will have. By trail braking into the tight corner, having lots of weight on the front tires and little on the rears, your car will have less traction. But the tradeoff is usually a good one: you're giving up some overall traction in return for changing the direction of the car. In tight, slow corners, that's a good compromise.

Let's look at the fast, sweeping corner. With the greater radius, getting the car to change direction is of less importance. What's most important is overall traction, so that you're able to carry as much speed as possible through the corner. What's the solution? Much less trail braking, possibly none at all. Earlier and maybe quicker release of the brake pedal. In fact, with many fast corners, you want to be completely off the brake pedal by the time you start turning the steering wheel to initiate the turn.

In this case, with a fast corner, you're better off focusing on maximizing overall traction and giving up something when it comes to using weight transfer to help change the direction of the car. Your goal is to keep the car—the platform—as flat and balanced as possible, from the nanosecond that you turn into the corner to enable you to carry as much speed through it.

As you get faster and faster when driving on the track and you begin chasing faster lap times, you'll fight a tendency to rush fast corners. You'll want to leave your braking later and later, and brake harder and harder, trying to eke out a little faster lap time. But as we just learned, with fast sweeping corners, this is not the best way to drive.

When approaching a fast corner with an eye to improving your overall lap time, make your speed adjustment early (whether that adjustment is simply a lift of the throttle or application of the brakes). How early should it be? A good guideline is to do it early enough so that you're able to get back to accelerating by the time you initiate your turn into the corner. Compare when you begin pressing on the gas pedal to when you begin turning the steering wheel. If you're

SPEED SECRET

Adapt your brake release and turning of the steering wheel to the shape of the corner.

not getting to the throttle until after turning into the corner, make your speed adjustment earlier next lap.

This is a guideline, not a hard and fast rule—and there are always exceptions to the rules. But if you start with this guideline, then move your speed adjustment zone in and out a little either way and notice which results in a faster time through that segment of the track, you'll figure out the best way.

Every corner requires a different level of compromise between changing the car's direction through the use of managing weight transfer (trail braking—the timing and rate of release of the brakes) and balancing the car to maximize its traction level to carry as much speed through the corner as possible.

Many drivers approach every corner the same, but the best drivers adapt their technique to suit the corner. As you become more aware of the timing and rate of release of the brakes, how that affects weight transfer and the ability to change your car's direction, and reading the track's shape and direction, you'll be better at finding the ideal compromise—and be in a position to go faster more consistently.

BALANCE

To reinforce what I said above, the smoother you drive, the better balanced your car will be. The better balanced your car is—and by this I mean having the weight distributed as close to equally over all four tires—the more grip it will have. The more grip your tires have, the faster you can drive. And that's why keeping your car balanced is so important.

Having said that, there are times where changing the balance away from equal distribution over all four tires can be used to your advantage. For example, as you enter a tight corner, slowly releasing the brakes so that more weight is over the front tires will help your car turn more responsively. It will help rotate the car, changing direction more sharply.

With experience, you'll use your car's balance to make it do what you want.

WHEN SMOOTH IS NOT FAST

"You're so smooth . . . except when you apply the brakes. You really hit them hard." That's a comment I've heard more than once after giving a sport, track day, or HPDE driver a ride around the track. Variations of this comment come from the same people after riding with anyone I would call a "pro driver."

I'm the first to preach the message that smooth is fast. But there's one place where many drivers who don't race for a living are just a little too smooth, and that's where they initially apply the brakes.

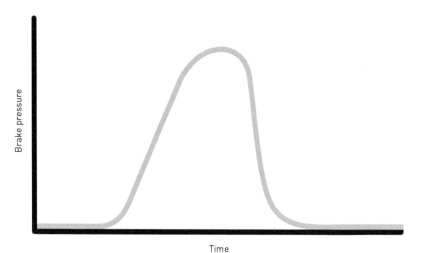

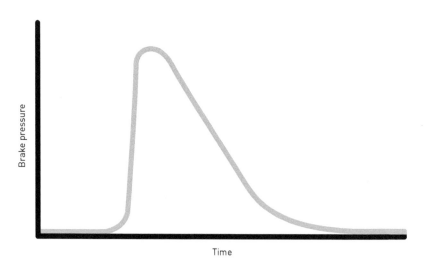

This shows two brake-pressure traces, indicating the amount of pressure that is being applied to the brakes. The top illustration shows the way most drivers use the brakes while approaching a traffic light, and the bottom illustration shows how a high-performance driver brakes (especially on a racetrack) —the initial application of the brakes is quick and hard.

Use a hard initial application of the brakes and gradually bleed off the pressure.

As I wrote earlier, we learn from driving on the street to focus on the end-of-braking point, and to apply the brakes appropriately to stop where we want. That's the positive of what can be learned driving on the street.

The negative is the tendency—and ultimately, the building of a habit—to squeeze the brakes on a little too slowly when driving on the street. In fact, most drivers brake relatively lightly when they first apply pressure to the pedal approaching a traffic light, and then gradually increase the pressure as the car travels through the "brake zone," finally coming to a complete stop with the hardest pressure on the pedal.

That's the opposite of how you should brake on the racetrack—and in most high-performance driving situations. You want to spike up the initial pressure as quickly as possible to the maximum amount that the car and tires can handle, then slightly bleed off the pressure as the car slows (and the grip level is reduced). Finally, you should gently ease off as you trail brake into the turn.

You can squeeze the brakes on very, very quickly, and hard. Most drivers of production-based track or race cars don't apply that pressure hard enough or fast enough. Drivers of cars with lots of aerodynamic downforce learn that they have more grip at high speed (due to the aero), but also that it reduces as the car slows—and they learn to apply hard initial pressure to the brake pedal.

That's what many sport/track day/HPDE drivers notice when riding with someone with much more experience. If they use it themselves, they find they turn faster lap times.

11 ROAD DRIVING

Wouldn't it be wonderful if we could spend all our time driving on racetracks? If there's a heaven, that's my vision of it.

Unfortunately, I don't know anyone who drives on a track more than they do on the street. I suspect there is someone out there who has arranged his or her life so that they don't drive much on the street, spending most of their time driving on tracks. I want to meet that person!

Since we drive on the street more than a track, how do we take advantage of that? And how can we also be the best driver that we can be while on the street? That's the focus of this chapter.

I'm going to suggest two things:

- Use street driving to make yourself a better track driver. Your entire focus when driving on the street is to develop the skills, techniques, and mindset to be a better driver when you get to the track.
- Take every part of your street driving—from inching along in rush-hour traffic to avoiding collisions—and do them at the highest possible level. That is driving at a high-performance level.

Almost everything I've written in this book can be applied to street driving, all while obeying the law. With that in mind, I'm going to focus this chapter on my second point: being the best high-performance driver you can be while driving on the street.

READING THE ROAD

One thing that every driver does naturally is what I call "reading the road." As you drive, you constantly note and evaluate the shape, layout, and condition of the road ahead. You do this without even thinking about it. It's one of the most important things you do while driving.

The more effectively you read the road, the safer you'll be. Let's take a look at just some of the things you can do.

If you're driving a winding country road or a mountain highway, one of the most difficult tasks you face is knowing which way the road curves on the other side of a hillcrest or around a bend. A simple glance at the tree line or the telephone poles can give you a hint about the direction and inclination on the other side of the hill.

High-performance drivers are constantly reading the road, looking for clues that will tell them what's up ahead.

At night, shadows will give you a hint of upcoming bumps and rises. Light travels in a straight line, so when you see a shadow, the road is dropping below your headlights at that point. Likewise, if the surface is gathering more light, it is rising. Since oil and antifreeze leaking from cars are more likely to be shaken off and onto the ground by a bump, you can assume that where there is dark, stained roadway, there is a bump—to be avoided, if possible.

Watch for uphill, downhill, banked, and off-camber corners. They will have a considerable effect on the acceleration, deceleration, and turning of any car. Use these to your advantage—and conversely, attempt to minimize their disadvantages. Just remember that a car going uphill or turning on a banked corner has better traction than one going downhill or on an off-camber corner.

Traction capabilities can and should be checked at very low speeds whenever possible—especially in adverse conditions. When it is safe to do so, brake heavily to determine where the braking traction limit is under these particular conditions. Don't wait until you're approaching a stop sign or an emergency situation to find out the road is a little icy! That's too late.

Try to avoid braking or accelerating heavily when driving over painted road markings—especially in the wet—as these are often very slippery. Also, watch for leaves on the roadway. Driving on wet leaves can be like driving on ice.

A final thought on this is to look far ahead, read the road, and watch for

SPEED SECRET

Read the road.

changing conditions. Most importantly, think about how the environment you're driving through will affect you and your vehicle.

READING OTHER DRIVERS

One of the things I enjoy while driving is watching other drivers, particularly their driving positions. This not only adds a little entertainment: it also helps me be better prepared for whatever actions they may take. It adds another little challenge to driving, which helps me keep my concentration. I love trying to predict what a driver is going to do just by the look of their vehicle and how they sit in it.

This is something that some drivers already do. Either they were taught this, or they learned it by trial and error. It's what I call "reading other drivers." You may be surprised how many potential crashes can be avoided by paying attention to the way fellow motorists act.

To begin reading other drivers, note their position behind the wheel. Are they sitting upright and alert? How are they holding onto the steering wheel—or are they? If the driver is talking on a cell phone (hands free or not), reading something, or drinking a cup of coffee, give them a bit more room—they're going to need it.

Of course, the funniest thing to notice is drivers' hand positions on the steering wheel. There is the "praying mantis," where the driver has both hands together at the very top of the wheel. There's the "crotch grip," where the driver holds the wheel at the very bottom (6 o'clock). This is often accompanied by the right arm over the back of the passenger seat or the left arm out the window and holding onto the roof or side mirror (are they afraid they're going to blow off in the wind?). Then there's the "bicycle racer," the driver who holds the wheel with both hands on the cross spokes.

None of these positions are effective in controlling a vehicle. They represent habits. And what they tell you is that this driver has less control of his or her vehicle than you do. You're going to have to take extra care around that driver.

I also like to note other drivers' mirror positions and how often they use them. I specifically like to check if I can see the other driver's eyes in the mirror. If I can't, I know two things: first, they can't see me (I'll either back off or speed up a little to move into a position so they can see me); and second, they haven't adjusted their mirrors correctly—if they had, there would not be any blind spots. Watching to

Reading other drivers—but not getting caught up in their emotions—is another skill great drivers use.

see how often other drivers check their mirrors can be both frightening and educational. Many drivers will drive for miles without even the slightest glance in their mirrors. Again, this provides you with a hint about whether you want to drive near them.

Notice the condition of the other car. Sometimes, but not always, this can be an indication of how a person feels about driving. If the vehicle is uncared for, the driver may also not take good care of his or her own driving mentally. A telltale sign that I always look for: gigantic scrapes or other crash damage. This is not always the sign of a bad driver, but I certainly give these cars extra attention when they're nearby.

Also consider whether drivers are alone or have passengers. If they're alone, they may be starting to doze off—particularly on the open highway or in rush-hour traffic. If they have passengers, they may be busy talking to them. Either way, they may not be paying attention as much as they should.

Watch for drivers who wander all over their lane, or those who tailgate; give drivers like this more room. Remember to factor in the traffic volume and road conditions as well. What may be acceptable driving on the open highway on a sunny day may not be appropriate on a snowy day in rush hour.

Driving in traffic should really be like working as part of a team. If all drivers pay attention to one another and work together, traffic will flow much better. As I mentioned early in this book, collaborative driving should be a goal.

Watching and reading other drivers also reminds me of some bad habits I may be developing. By observing others, I can correct my errors before they become habits. Give it a try.

TRAFFIC SKILLS/TIPS

With today's traffic getting heavier each day, driving safely requires more concentration than ever before. In fact, alertness may just be the most important key to surviving our hectic traffic. That, and a few basic, common-sense tips. Take a look at these.

Stop far enough behind other cars for you to have an escape route. When coming to a stop behind another vehicle at an intersection, make sure you have room to move in case of an emergency. If the vehicle behind you isn't slowing down (perhaps about to rear-end you), you have the option to pull forward or off to the side. A good rule of thumb is to stop so that you can still see the bottom of the rear tires of the car in front; this should mean you're back far enough so that you can still move out of the way in an emergency. Plus, if the vehicle in front of you should stall or have problems, you have room to get around it.

Always stop far enough back from the vehicle in front of you so that you have a view of the bottom of its rear tires. This gives you a little room to escape in an emergency.

Check the rearview mirror when you stop. Keep an eye on the vehicle behind you until it has also come to a complete stop. This allows you to move out of its way if it is not going to stop in time (of course, you should also have given yourself room behind the car in front of you). Many rear-enders could be avoided if only you kept an eye on the rearview mirror.

Watch for "stale" green lights and/or pedestrian cross signals. As you approach intersections, note whether the light has been green since you first noticed it or green for quite some time. If so, it is "stale," and may change to yellow soon. Also watch the pedestrian cross signals; if it's a "Don't Walk" signal, your light is bound to turn yellow shortly. You can assume a stale green will change to yellow or red by the time you get there. In this case, cover the brake pedal and be prepared to stop.

Look before you turn. Before turning off a main road onto a side street, take a good look at where you're going. Watch for pedestrians or other cars that might impede your travel. When pulling out of a parking lot or driveway—or crossing a sidewalk—watch for pedestrians, particularly on your right. Don't just look for the traffic coming from the left; if you do, you will probably not notice the pedestrians.

Stay back from stop lines. When approaching an intersection, stop so that you can see the entire crosswalk or stop line. This enables you to see small children in the crosswalk and it will give you a more complete view of the traffic. Many times, children will dash across a crosswalk while you are looking to the left (checking for oncoming traffic); if you are sitting on top of the crosswalk, you may not see them. Stop before the crosswalk, then proceed forward—checking for traffic—and enter the intersection.

I often see people drive up to a side street and stop well beyond the stop line at the intersection. They end up sitting there for a long time, as they have gone beyond the signal triggering mechanism embedded in the roadway. Not only that, but they are now sitting across the crosswalk, making it inconvenient and dangerous for pedestrians. This practice is also against the law.

The Don't Walk signal is one indication that the green light you're approaching may change to yellow very soon.

I recall someone telling me a story about a driver of a small truck doing the same thing—stopping beyond the stop line, with the nose of the vehicle in the crosswalk. In this case, the driver was trying to make a right turn. As he looked to his left to check for oncoming traffic, a pedestrian began to cross the road from the right. Just as the pedestrian got in front of the truck, she dropped something. She bent over to pick it up. As that happened, the driver began his turn around the right corner, hitting the pedestrian. If the driver had stopped back from the crosswalk, he would have seen her.

The proper way, of course, is to stop with the nose of your vehicle even with the marked stop line or so that you can see the leading edge of the marked crosswalk. If there are no lines, then stop so that the nose of your vehicle doesn't protrude beyond an imaginary line connecting the edge of the cross street.

Check left and right at intersections. Before moving away from a stop at an intersection, or while driving through one, check traffic to the left and right. Never assume the stop sign or signal light is going to stop another vehicle from unlawfully entering an intersection. Usually, all that's needed is a quick glance, mainly using your peripheral vision.

Use your turn signals. No matter how obvious it is to *you* where you're going, it may not be to other drivers around you. Always use your turn signals to indicate where you're going.

The writer C. S. Lewis said, "Integrity is doing the right thing, even when no one is watching." Even when no one is around, use your turn signal, as not doing so builds a bad habit. Have integrity as a driver.

Wait before moving. Count "one-thousand-one" before removing your foot from the brake pedal and following another car into an intersection (from a stop). With your foot on the brakes, your brake lights will keep the car behind you in place until you have room to move through the intersection. Often, if you take off immediately after the car in front, the car following will tailgate you through the intersection—a problem if you have to stop suddenly. Also, taking some extra time before entering the intersection will result in a good space cushion between you and the car in front.

Wait to cross blocked intersections. In heavy, bumper-to-bumper traffic, do not move into the intersection unless you can clear it before the traffic light turns yellow.

Drive in the best lane. How you position your vehicle in its lane and in relationship to other vehicles on the road is a critical factor in how safely you drive.

Position your car as though there is a bubble around you. At speed, on a freeway, this bubble becomes longer and more narrow; in city traffic it's rounder, as there is more activity to the sides of your car. Protect the bubble!

It's vital to remember to drive where you can be seen by other drivers. Don't travel in another driver's blind spot (usually the area just alongside the rear fender). Check it. If you can't see the other driver in his mirrors, he or she can't see you. This mirror check is an especially important tool when following a large truck. Either speed up or slow down a little to adjust your position relative to the other vehicle, so that you can be seen.

Often, when following a large truck, your vision of traffic lights, other cars, intersections, and so on, is restricted. Again, back off and leave more room between you and the truck so you can see properly.

On a two-lane city street, which is the best lane to travel in? The left lane, or right lane? Well, there is no one *best* lane. But by looking well ahead, you should be able to determine which lane is best at that moment. Sometimes, the left lane is the best to avoid the parked cars and vehicles pulling out of side streets. At other times, the right lane is better to keep everything moving. The key is to keep your eyes up and be aware of the rhythm of the traffic flow. Constantly look ahead and reevaluate which is the best lane to drive in.

On a highway, it's a different story: stay in the right lane unless passing another vehicle. Too many drivers get in the left lane and just stay there, regardless of whether they're passing someone. This often results in building the frustration level of the drivers following until they do something stupid that endangers everyone, including the driver blocking the left lane.

Drive with an escape route. Don't trap yourself in a position where you can't make an evasive move to avoid an emergency. Often, that only means moving a few feet forward or backward in relation to the other vehicles around you.

It's important to leave yourself room to move. Always position your vehicle so that you have an escape route in case of an emergency. Be sure to have room at the rear, sides, and front. This may mean speeding up or slowing down just slightly to create a safety zone. Don't

trap yourself into a position where you can't make an evasive move to avoid a problem.

Don't turn your wheels until you begin to move. Imagine sitting at a signal light waiting to make a left turn. If you have your front wheels turned to the left—anticipating the turn—and someone rear-ends you: what's going to happen? The impact will knock you into oncoming traffic, making the crash even worse. To avoid this, point your wheels straight until it's time to move.

Brake early and smoothly. In traffic, brake early to communicate to drivers behind that you are slowing or stopping. If you leave your braking late and then have to brake hard, you're almost asking to be rear-ended. By braking early and smoothly, your brake lights will warn following drivers.

Use lane discipline. Many drivers seem to pay no attention to the lane markings on the roadway; lately, this seems to be getting worse. I know I'm talking to the wrong people here (I imagine most readers of this book are very conscientious about their driving), but a little reminder can't hurt.

SPEED

Here's a subject that should stir up some controversy: speeding. How fast should you drive? The posted speed limit, "with the flow of traffic," "whatever feels comfortable," or "whatever it takes to get there on time"?

My goal in this section is simply to get you to think about those answers. I'm not going to tell you what speed to drive on the street; I'll leave that to you, but I hope you make a decision after thinking about what I present here.

First of all, I think most will agree that excessive speed is a problem. But what is "excessive"? I think many drivers don't realize how just a little extra speed (sometimes as little as 5 miles per hour more) can put you into that "excessive" zone.

Many people feel they are good drivers—good enough to control their car and the traffic situation around them, which gives them the capacity to exceed the speed limit as they wish.

As someone who has spent the last forty years driving cars very fast, my driving skills are probably as good as most drivers on the street—maybe even better. Generally, though, I don't feel it is safe to exceed the speed limit by much. Why? Because I know where the limits of my vehicle are, and I understand that, if I exceed them, there's a good chance I'll be involved in a crash. I've seen firsthand what a nominal increase in speed can do.

Plus—and this may be the most important point—I don't know how good the drivers around me are. I would bet there are at least a few who are not very good!

This is not to say that I never exceed the speed limit: sometimes I do, but not on purpose. I try to stick close to the speed limit. Like any other human, though, I make mistakes. And when I do, I try to correct it by slowing down.

A speed-limit sign is just one way of determining what is a safe speed to drive (and it's the legal way).

Driving "with the flow of traffic" is actually recommended by some—even some driving schools. However, it's usually people looking for an excuse to drive a little faster than the speed limit who recommend this.

My question is, who's setting the speed of "the flow of traffic"? Someone in a hurry to get to work? Drivers who feel they have the skill to drive 20 miles per hour over the speed limit? I suggest we start to think more about our own speed, stay a little closer to the posted speed limit, and set our own "flow of traffic."

Here's an interesting fact: on an average 30-minute daily commute in an urban area, the overall time saved by driving "with the flow" (or even with excessive speed), instead of sticking to the speed limit, is less than a minute. Try it and see for yourself.

You must decide whether it's worth the extra minute to put yourself and others at a much greater risk of crashing—not to mention the cost, hassle, and other problems that come with getting caught while speeding.

Over the past few years, I've had the opportunity to see the results of speeding—especially the disadvantages. More importantly, I've seen for myself that there is practically no *advantage* to speeding. So why do it, when the *disadvantages* outweigh the advantages?

Let's consider this issue from a vehicle dynamics point of view: we often face the challenge of driving in varying conditions—rain, sunshine, snow, fog, you name it. Fortunately, these changing conditions usually only affect one driving variable—speed. Different conditions should affect the speed we drive, but how many of us really know how much we should slow down when conditions change for the worse, and how many of us actually do it?

Did you know that the average car with average tires on a wet road has only about 70 percent of the traction of the same vehicle on a dry road? This means it will take 30 percent more room to stop on a wet road if traveling at the same speed. If it were safe to travel at 60 miles per hour when the road was dry, from a pure physics perspective you should actually slow down to about 50 or so miles per hour when it's raining.

How about in snow and ice? A car may only get about 30 to 40 percent of dry traction in snow, and less than 15 percent on ice. Again, if these are the conditions on a road where you normally drive at 60, you should do only about 20 miles per hour in snow, and less than half that on ice.

Of course, your tires are only one of the contributing factors here. In fact, these percentages are strictly a function of tire traction, and they only serve as rough guides.

Let's take another look at speed from yet another angle.

As I mentioned earlier, there's a certain level of risk every time you drive. On a nice, sunny day on an open highway with little traffic around, the risk level is relatively low. However, when traffic volume is heavier, the risk level increases, just as it does when it rains, when it's dark, when your mind is on something other than driving, and so on.

The most important skill that we as drivers must develop is the *accurate assessment* of the risk level in a given situation, followed by the conscious adjustment of our driving (speed, concentration) to compensate.

As you approach a section of road with heavier traffic volume, if it starts to rain or other such factors come into play, a good driver should realize that the risk level has just gone up. He or she should react by slowing down and paying more attention.

The problem is that many drivers don't perceive that the risk level is as high as it really is, or they believe they're such good drivers that they can "handle it."

It amazes me how fast people drive in poor, high-risk-level conditions. A while ago, I was driving over a bridge at night in the rain (poor visibility), with heavy winds. I was driving a new car (good tires, ABS, stability control, etc.) with both hands on the steering wheel, thinking about my driving. A driver passed me doing about 70 miles per hour (10 over the speed limit) in a much older car, obviously in poor mechanical condition. The driver had one hand on the steering wheel and was turning around to talk to passengers in the rear.

Do you think this driver had accurately assessed the level of risk in driving at that particular moment? I don't think so. I'm not sure he was even thinking about where he was. In fact, he was just a fraction away from disaster. If anything else had happened (someone hitting the brakes or quickly changing lanes in front of him), it would have put him over the limit and evolved into a crash. He had no cushion, room for error—nothing in reserve.

You can talk all day long about "if you have the driving skill, you can drive faster than the speed limit," but driving skill is only part of it. Risk level is the

SPEED SECRET

Drive at an appropriate speed to match the risk level at that very moment.

critical factor. Being able to accurately assess and respond to the constantly changing risk level is the key. The posted speed limit is a good guide for doing that. Think about it!

As you can tell, I believe that driving above the posted speed limit is asking for trouble. Still, "speeding" is only part of the problem. The real issue is *why* people speed.

Generally, most people drive above the posted speed limit because they don't realize the consequences. They don't recognize the risks involved. They feel they can handle the speed. If you asked them if they were safe at the speed they were driving—no matter how much over the posted speed limit they were—practically every one of them would say "yes." Very few drivers deliberately drive unsafely.

Then there are those drivers who just don't think about it at all. They're often the ones who drive at the same speed, whether they're on an open road with no traffic on a sunny day, on a crowded freeway at night in the pouring rain, or on an icy road on a snowy winter day. They don't even think about how the conditions can make driving riskier.

Without considering the legal aspects, speed limits are a guideline. They are the best guideline drivers have in determining the varying conditions we drive in. If the road is in a more congested area, the speed limit is reduced. If the shape or layout of the road makes driving riskier, the speed limit is reduced. If it opens up to a multi-lane highway, the speed limit is raised. If the multi-lane highway has entrance and exit ramps (as opposed to intersections), the speed limit is raised again.

The posted speed limit does not take into account the following, though: weather conditions; the amount of traffic around you; your own concentration or distraction level; the skill and awareness levels of the drivers around you; your vehicle's condition and its ability to handle the demands put on it in an emergency; and so on. It's your job to consider these factors and determine whether you're safe, even driving at the speed limit.

Most of the time, the posted speed limit is a great guideline, leaving you with a little in reserve for the unexpected. But it's still up to you to react to changing conditions and risk levels.

I would love to see speed limits raised. But, especially with the increased traffic levels we face today, combined with the skill and awareness levels of the average motorist, I don't think it would be safe. The best advice for safe driving is still to stick to the posted speed limit while remaining mindful of the constantly changing conditions.

One last theory about speeding: for the moment, let's ignore the posted legal speed limit, instead considering "inappropriate speed." This is speed that's too fast for the conditions (such as weather, traffic volume, visibility) or other factors (such as your vehicle condition, your mental state). Nearly everyone would agree that inappropriate speed is dangerous.

At what point, though, does driving speed become inappropriate? In many cases, unfortunately, it's speed that many people drive, because of something I call the "Speed Peter Principle."

You know the Peter Principle, when a person is promoted until they become incompetent for the job. For example, a salesperson of the year may be promoted to sales manager; the best mechanic at the shop becomes the service manager; the best computer programmer becomes the computer department manager. This is great if the individual has good management skills, but, without these, they'll do a poor job in their new position while wasting their real talent. They are working beyond their capabilities.

Most drivers choose the speed they drive in much the same fashion. They increase their speed to the point where they're just beyond the level of their competency. In this case, they drive beyond the point of being fully in control, on the edge of being out of control. These people are driving beyond their capabilities.

Many would argue with this position: a good number of drivers on the road don't think they are on the verge of being out of control. Often, they're correct— if they're the only drivers on the road. When you factor in all the traffic, not to mention the other distractions and environmental conditions, most of these drivers don't realize how close they are to running into serious problems.

Sometimes I find myself on a stretch of road where there is very little traffic, in nice weather, and I wish the posted speed limit was higher. But I'm sure most people will agree that, in today's urban areas, it's rare to find a street that's open for driving, not crowded with vehicles. I would bet that at least half the driving we do in this country is in less-than-ideal conditions—night, rain, low visibility, and worse.

That's why it's easy to fall into the Speed Peter Principle.

If you don't mind being on the verge of a problem all the time, then carry on. Just be sure you can handle the consequences. If you don't want to fall victim to the Peter Principle, ease off a little.

I'm never going to influence the speed you drive by preaching to you, though: you need to determine how quickly you drive for yourself.

Speed. Think about it. More importantly, indulge your desire for speed in a place where it's safe: on a racetrack.

12 TRACK DRIVING

You've bought your dream car, or something close to it, and now you want to track it. Yes! I was hoping you'd want to do that, and even hoping this book inspired you a little to do so.

Unless you intend to go racing, there are two types of events that are of interest to you: HPDE and track-day events.

We've already mentioned high performance driver education (HPDE). The "E" is sometimes mistakenly thought to stand for "experience" or "event," but the industry-accepted use of HPDE is to cover an *educational* event. The other activity, a "track day," occurs when no educational component is scheduled as part of the event: it's just drivers driving their cars on a track according to a structured schedule. The difference between the two is that an HPDE is about learning to be a better driver, while a track day event focuses on the fun aspects of driving around a track (of course, you'll often learn things while having fun on a track, too).

Most events offer a combination of education and fun, so the terms do get mixed up and overlapped at times. In fact, many events start drivers with an educational focus, and, as they gain experience, these drivers receive less and less education, with the focus tending more toward just lapping the track.

Taking your car to a racetrack to drive is one of the most fun things you'll ever do. And you'll learn more about high-performance driving in fifteen minutes there than you will in fifteen years of driving on the street!

In reality, it's almost impossible to drive around a track and not at least think about improving. The constant challenge to "do it better" brings drivers back to the track time after time, a bit like a drug addiction. As one of my favorite automotive writers, Peter Egan, once said, "Racing makes a heroin addiction look like a vague wish for something salty."

I'm warning you now: track driving is addictive.

While there are many different formats for HPDE and track-day events, all feature a few common elements. First, you show up early at the track with your car well prepared—at least you should. A meeting starts the day off, with the person leading the event providing an overview of the schedule and rules. The attending drivers will have already been split into groups, ranging from first-timers and inexperienced drivers to intermediates and experienced drivers. Each group will go in a different direction: the newbies head to a classroom session, where they will learn the basics of high-performance driving (an abbreviated version of the content of Chapters 3 through 8 in this book); experienced drivers head directly onto the track; and the intermediates receive a short briefing and some time to prepare for their session on track.

Most organizations have "run groups" (novice, intermediate, advanced—often referred to by letters or colors), and each group is on track for twenty to thirty minutes at a time, followed by the next group, then the next, and so on throughout the day. As part of the HPDE program, the novice group will have short classroom sessions before and in between their on-track sessions.

TECHNICAL INSPECTION

Before the drivers' meeting at the beginning of the day, your car will usually undergo a technical inspection—having it "teched." This entails having someone look your car over and give it his or her blessing that it's safe to drive on track.

Even though they should have good knowledge of what a car needs to pass, don't rely on this person to be the expert and catch every problem with your car. They're not responsible for your car: you are. They're looking for the obvious—tire condition, wheels torqued, battery not falling out of the engine compartment, no fluids leaking, and you have the appropriate safety equipment installed and ready to wear. If your brake pads are worn out, the tech inspection is unlikely to catch that; it's up to you to ensure that the basic components are safe for use under the strains of track driving.

Not all HPDE/track day event organizers perform this tech inspection, as they count on you to make sure your car is safe and reliable. If your car breaks down during the day, you're out of luck—and out the money you spent to participate all day.

SAFETY EQUIPMENT

Speaking of safety equipment, you'll need a helmet, and there are specific regulations for its standards. I'm not going to cover them here because they're updated every few years, and different organizations have different standards. Check with the organization you're going to run with to make sure your helmet meets their rules.

In fact, different organizations have different rules for head-and-neck restraint systems (i.e., HANS devices, hybrid, etc.), seat belts/harnesses, rollover protection, whether convertibles are allowed, and other safety-related issues. Check with the organization you're running with to see that you have everything in place.

This is one of the most important parts I cover in this book, so pay attention: get the best helmet you can afford (and stretch to afford an even better one). As the saying goes, "if you have a five-dollar head, use a five-dollar helmet." How much is protecting your head worth to you and your family?

A head and neck restraint system is as important as a helmet. Devices are available for use with either a standard three-point seat belt (the one your car came with) or with five- or six-point performance driving harnesses.

Some of these rules and regulations (and the cost of a good-quality helmet and head and neck restraint system) may be off-putting and make you think twice about getting involved with track driving. Don't let them bother you. One thing I can guarantee is that organizers of the HPDE/track-day event will do everything they can to accommodate you and make your experience at the track safe, fun, educational, rewarding, and even relaxing.

Relaxing? You might wonder how driving very fast around a racetrack could be relaxing, but those who've been involved in the sport for any length of time will tell you it is. Often, it can be the most relaxing thing they ever do. When you're driving on track, you're focused; nothing else matters. Everything else in your life that may distract you and cause you stress goes out the window when you're driving on the track.

TRACK EVENT ORGANIZERS

The organizations that run HPDE and track day events fall into one of two categories: nonprofit car clubs, and for-profit businesses. See the Appendix for more details.

SPEED SECRET

Get and use the best safety equipment possible.

Bear in mind that the marque clubs won't stop you from attending their events if you don't have the "right" brand of car. In fact, they'll likely welcome you with open arms. Sure, they love their Audis, Miatas, Corvettes, or whatever, but what they love most are fellow car enthusiasts, and especially ones who love to drive. So feel free to show up at a Mustang Club event driving a Škoda!

You can't go wrong in deciding between a nonprofit car club event or an HPDE put on by a for-profit business. They have their pros and cons, and, as with most things, the cream rises to the top. Read the reviews on social media about the various events and organizations, as that'll help you decide which organization you want to drive and learn with.

My strong recommendation is that you begin with an organization that prides itself in the educational side of things. If the organizer is simply touting how much track time they provide but doesn't talk about learning, education, and helping you improve over time, I'd look elsewhere. Obviously, the amount of time you get on the track is important, but seat time for the sake of seat time is not what you need, especially in the beginning. What you need most is quality seat time, and that means having quality instruction.

While there isn't much to choose between the best HPDE and track day organizers, there are some organizers who don't fall into the "best" category. Typically, these are run by someone who is simply pulling a group of drivers together to go drive around a track; education is not their focus. I'd stay away from these.

In addition to looking for a focus on education, the main factors to consider when choosing an organization to run with are their instructors and overall culture. Some emphasize the social aspect more than others, some are more structured with their schedule and rules, some have a more competitive environment, some are more focused on the car than the driver, and so on. You need to find what suits your approach to the sport.

INSTRUCTORS

The instructors make or break an organization and an event. They're the ones communicating the culture, and they're going to make the difference between you having fun and learning or not. And more importantly, staying safe. Many organizations trade track time with instructors for their services, and a few pay them in the more traditional way. Keep in mind that you most often get what you pay for.

Selection, training, and experience separate the best instructors from the rest. Too often, the selection criteria for an instructor is whether that person is a fast driver. This makes no more sense than assuming a good salesperson is also a good sales department manager, or that the best mechanic is a good shop manager. Driving fast and instructing are two very different skills. While many organizations will tell you that they select their instructors based on their ability to communicate and connect with students (very important traits), many are chosen based on availability, the amount of experience they have driving on track, and whether they're part of "the" group.

Ask around.

THE CAR YOU DRIVE

Back to that dream car of yours.

Unless it's an early 3 Series BMW, an early 1970s Porsche 911, a Mazda Miata, or Subaru BRZ (or something similar), don't take it to the track. In fact, if it's equipped with tires wider than 225, and if it has stability control, traction control, adaptive cruise control, and any other type of control that requires a computer, trade in your dream car for one of the four I mentioned and learn how to drive.

Do I sound like an old fuddy-duddy, reminiscing about the old days and how things used to be? That's not the point. The point is that modern cars, with all of their driver aids and incredibly high traction levels, take away from your experience of learning to drive. They do so much for you, often hiding or masking the mistakes that great drivers use to learn and improve. They make drivers think they're controlling the car, when it's the technology that's controlling it.

In addition, despite the safety these systems provide, they still have to work within the laws of physics. If physics says you're going to spin off the track or roadway, even with all of the control systems doing their behind-the-scenes magic for you, you're going to go off the track or roadway—at a higher speed!

(This reminds me of the saying, "Four-wheel-drive off-road vehicles are great. They go further into the forest or mud before you get stuck!").

Don't get me wrong: I love all the technology in modern cars, and I'm a big proponent of them. But they have their time and place, and if you really, truly want to learn how to drive at your best, you'll do better with a car that doesn't include a lot of technological help. You'll learn more in a car with lesser performance, one with fewer systems designed to save your bacon when you mess up.

You should spend at least two seasons of driving on the track in a car *without* these driver aids, learning how to sense and control the limits of your car. Then, once you've made enough mistakes and learned from them, take your dream car with all of its "nannies" to the track.

Okay, if you already have a car with some or all of the things I said you don't want to learn with—and you don't want to trade it in for something simpler— you'll have to work with what you've got. You're going to have to learn to drive your car with all of the driver aids.

The question then becomes, what you should do with those driver aids when at the track? Should you leave them on, or should you turn them off?

That's the 64-bit question!

With many cars, this isn't an option: they don't allow you to turn any of the safety systems off (unless you have a fourteen-year-old hacker on hand to break into the system, which I don't recommend).

DRIVER AIDS—ON OR OFF?

Before I answer that question, understand this is a controversial subject with the organizers of track events. Some have policies that state you can never turn anything off, others leave it up to the individual driver or instructor to decide, and some tell you to turn them all off. My goal here is not to go against or support any of these policies or procedures; you should respect and follow their policies. My goal is to discuss the pros and cons, and provide my opinion, based on what is best *strictly from a learning perspective*.

ABS

ABS is a system you can't turn off, and there's no real reason to do so. Tick. No need to discuss. Or is there?

Should you use ABS when braking for a corner on a racetrack? That depends on the car you're driving and its brake system. In most cars, it's best to brake just slightly before activating ABS, when you want to slow at the maximum rate. (Remember, there are times when braking at less than the limit is a good thing, and that's especially true if you decide to drive at something less than 10/10ths.) In many cars, if you fully engage the ABS, you'll slightly increase the length of the braking zone. In other cars with very high-end, performance-focused brake systems, using ABS is okay. If you want to drive the fastest lap possible, some cars give you what you want when you pounce on the brake pedal as hard as you can and hold it down, which fully engages the ABS.

As of this writing, these cars are in the minority. In other words, to turn the fastest lap possible you're better to keep the brakes just slightly under the pressure that activates the ABS—you'll be faster if you don't use ABS. How do you know which is best? You have to experiment with and without using the ABS.

Of course, this relates only to driving at the very limit, and most drivers don't need or want to push their cars that hard. After all, it raises the risk level and puts more wear and tear on your car. It may be best to stay just under the point in braking that will trigger the ABS.

How do you know when ABS has kicked in? First, you sense it in your foot, in the brake pedal: you can feel the pedal pulse. Sometimes, depending on the car, you can feel some of that pulsing of the brakes back through the steering wheel.

Traction and Stability Control
What about traction and stability control (which usually work together)? If you're able to drive the track at and slightly above the limit you've established for yourself (remember what I said in the Introduction about 8/10ths, 10/10ths, and so on?), knowing every single time when the traction or stability control system kicks in to help you, then you're ready to turn them off. This doesn't mean you have to—just that you're ready, since now you're aware of when the systems are helping you.

With some cars—especially performance cars with driver-focused instrument panels—you can leave the systems on and take notice of when the traction control light flashes, indicating that you're exceeding the limits of the system (but not necessarily the car). This can help a less-experienced driver be more gentle with inputs before deciding to turn the systems off.

If, on the other hand, an instructor riding with you points out how many times these systems saved you, then you should leave them on until you've become sensitive enough to know when they're helping you. It's not enough to rely on a little dash light coming on to warn you that the system is working. No, you need to be able to sense it with your butt and your ears, your kinesthetic and auditory senses.

Actually, there is a great practice strategy here. Drive the track with the sole focus being to recognize when any of the driver aids are being activated. If you feel the ABS kicking in—the vibration back through the pedal—then you know it's helping you avoid locking up the brakes. If you feel and hear the engine power being cut back, and/or the brakes on a wheel activated, then you know the traction and/or stability control systems are operating.

> **SPEED SECRET**
>
> When you can consistently recognize when the driver aids are assisting you—or even saving your butt from crashing—then and only then should you consider turning them off.

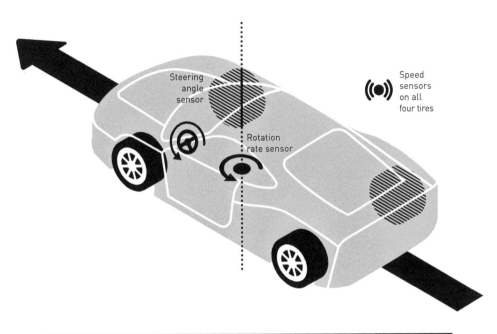

Steering angle sensor

Rotation rate sensor

Speed sensors on all four tires

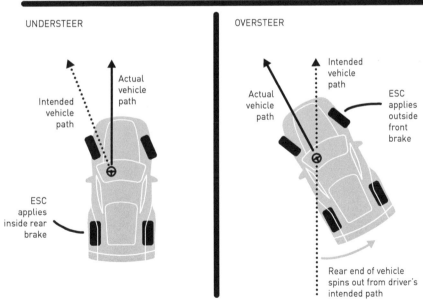

UNDERSTEER

Intended vehicle path

Actual vehicle path

ESC applies inside rear brake

OVERSTEER

Intended vehicle path

Actual vehicle path

ESC applies outside front brake

Rear end of vehicle spins out from driver's intended path

This illustrates how electronic stability control (ESC) works to assist with controlling understeer and oversteer.

By the way, if you notice that your rear brakes are overheating or that you're wearing one side out before the other, the stability control has been active. For example, if the way you're driving is causing the inside rear brake to activate over and over again to control understeer, the brakes on that corner of the car will run hotter and wear the pads much faster. Often, that's the first indication a driver has that the stability control system has been activated (even though they should have sensed it). Since road racing tracks have either more right than left turns, or vice versa (depending on which direction the track goes), it's not unusual for the brakes on one side of the car to wear out much faster than the other due to the activation of the stability control system.

When you decide to turn traction and stability control off, it's up to you to save your own butt from crashing, right? At this point, it's worth remembering what these driver aids are doing: they're activated when you've driven too fast for the conditions—track grip levels, weather, tire conditions, and the balance of your car (and therefore, its traction levels). They're activated when you're driving too fast, near or over the limits of the car in these conditions.

What does that tell you to do when you've turned them off? Ease off a little. If you continue to drive at the same pace that activated them, you're going to end up in some dicey situations—a skid, slide, or a spin. You may think you can control one of these deadly Ss, but that may not be possible. When you lose control, you and your car will most likely end up against a guardrail.

If you could turn off one system when you get to the track, it would be the adaptive cruise control and emergency braking assist, because together they automatically activate the brakes when they sense you're too close to another vehicle. This is an awesome system when driving on the street in traffic, but not so much on the track. If you happen to be driving through a corner closer to another car than the system likes, it will apply the brakes. If you're at or near the limits of the car, with the traction and stability control turned off, this could cause the car to spin.

You wouldn't suddenly apply the brakes in the middle of the corner, right? Remember from the vehicle dynamics chapter what this will do to your car: weight suddenly shifts forward, causing the rear of the car to have less traction, which could send your car spinning. At a minimum, it would mean quickly correcting for this imminent spin.

Unfortunately, many cars don't allow you to turn the adaptive cruise control off, which means that a car without this option is inappropriate for track driving.

SPEED SECRET

You'll always get more improvement out of your own driving than you will out of your car.

WHEN TO UPGRADE YOUR CAR

If you drive on a racetrack for a while, you'll eventually consider modifying and upgrading your car. This book isn't aimed at helping you improve your car's performance, other than by helping the "spacer" between the steering wheel and the seatback get better. My advice here focuses on the big picture, rather than on the details of how to modify your car.

Your approach to upgrading your car will have a big impact on your enjoyment of the sport, as well as how you improve your driving. Any modifications to your car should be approached in the following order:

1. Safety
2. Reliability
3. Performance

Unfortunately, many drivers take the opposite approach, spending serious money on making their cars faster. In the process, they make them less safe and less reliable. But if you're unsafe and your car breaks down all the time, you're not improving the car or having fun.

Perhaps the biggest question is when you should upgrade your car's performance. Part of the answer depends on your motivation for driving on a track. For some drivers, "playing" with their car's setup is a prime motivator; for them, upgrading may begin earlier than for a driver whose focus is on improving their driving skills. Either way, if you're driving far below the limits of your car, modifying it doesn't make a lot of sense; you'd be far better off focusing on developing your driving performance, not your car's.

When you can consistently drive your car near its limit, you'll have reached the appropriate time to consider upgrades. Having an outside observer—an instructor—provide honest feedback about your level of driving performance may save you a lot of money in the long run. If the feedback is aimed at improving your driving skills, rather than your car, do that first.

WHAT TO UPGRADE

Focus your first upgrades on making your car safer. You might consider installing a performance seat (which will also improve your driving performance), five- or six-point harnesses to hold you in place, and a roll bar or cage. Some drivers are reluctant to add these modifications to a car they drive on the street, so they skip this step and simply make their car faster. Think about that for a minute. Is it a good idea to make your car go faster without making it safer? Driving a car with no safety equipment at speeds much higher than some race cars that are equipped with safety equipment makes no sense. That's why making your car safer is the place to start.

Once you've made your car safer, look at what will make it more reliable. There's nothing worse than spending half your day working on your car at the track when you could be driving it. Start with the brakes, since they're often the weak link. You can think of upgrading brakes as a safety factor: first with fluid, then pads, ducting cooling air to them, and eventually better rotors and calipers.

As you can probably guess from my comments about the overall performance levels of modern high-performance cars, upgrading to ultra-sticky tires is not my top priority. Sure, you'll be able to get around a racetrack faster with them, but there are downsides to doing this. First, with stickier tires, you'll be going through corners even faster; that means an incident (such as a spin, a slide off the track, or hitting something) can have much higher consequences. Second, many drivers find that cars with the latest and stickiest tires are less fun to drive because they don't slide as much. Finally, the high g-force generated with these tires puts more load on every component in your car, adding to its wear and tear.

The details of what you do to upgrade your car's performance are up to you, but think about what's going to be the most fun and what will provide the best learning opportunity for you for every dollar you spend.

Finally, at some point you may think of upgrading to a designated track car, one that you don't drive on the street. Of course, that usually means investing in a trailer and tow vehicle to get to and from the track. It's at this point that many drivers "downgrade" from driving a high-end, expensive performance car to something less expensive and more fun. For example, a popular move is to replace a Porsche that's used as a daily driver with something like a Miata, which is built strictly for the track.

TRACK-DAY ADVICE

Get as much instruction as possible from as big a variety of instructors as possible.

Learn as much as you can before going to the track. Every second on the track costs you money, so get the most out of it. Prepare. See the Appendix to learn of more resources to help with this.

Understand what happens if something goes wrong and your car is damaged: you'll pay for it, no matter who's at fault. Unless you purchase insurance that is specifically meant for track driving, you're not covered. In other words, your usual insurance policy is unlikely to cover you if you damage your car on the track. Actually, that goes for you, personally, as well.

Start slow, and focus on learning.

Listen to your instructor. I know that some instructors are better than others, but in practically every situation, your instructor knows more about track driving than you do. You may even be a better driver, but your instructor will know how to get you around the track safely while you learn what you need to learn about track days.

Participating in a track day or HPDE event takes more than just driving skills. You have to learn the rules of the event, how the event is run, how to conduct yourself on and off track, the key personnel running the event, and even things as seemingly simple as the traffic flow direction in the paddock. I've seen too many drivers have their experience at an HPDE or track day ruined by the simple things that have little or nothing to do with actual driving skills.

Having an in-car instructor help you learn to drive on a track is one of the most effective things you can do to improve your driving.

Be prepared. Bring everything short of the kitchen sink with you to the track. Think you won't need that wrench or the extra bottles of water? Think again. Murphy's Law applies: if you bring it to the track, you won't need it; leave it at home and you'll be kicking yourself for not bringing it.

Bring extra clothing, drinks, snacks, and anything you might remotely need for your car. Make sure your gas tank is full when you arrive at the track, as you'll go through more fuel than you think. Too many drivers have their day—their learning and fun—cut short by not having something they should have brought.

In the weeks and days leading up to the event—well before heading to the track—have your car checked over, maintenance carried out, and everything prepared. If you show up and the event organizers decide your car is unfit for driving on the track, they'll send you home. Best-case scenario: they'll suggest you stick around and observe, sit in classroom sessions, and learn as much as you can.

Most organizations provide some form of classroom learning sessions at the track. If the event you're thinking about doesn't have this, or some other method of providing this training, I suggest you go to a different event where they *do* offer opportunities for learning. An HPDE or track day event without classroom training is a sign that the event organizer doesn't have your best interests in mind, only your money and a free-for-all.

With all of the information available in books and online these days, you should have all of the basic driving technique knowledge before you arrive at the track. You shouldn't rely only on what you'll learn in the at-track classroom sessions. Obviously, you're reading this book, so I'm preaching to the choir. But this book is just the beginning: there are more tools and resources you can use before heading to the track.

While it's critically important that the event you attend provides classroom training, understand that this is not the ideal learning environment for you.

If you're like just about every other person who's attended an HPDE or track day event, you're going to feel a little apprehensive, anxious, and nervous when you get to the track: these are not the ideal emotions for learning as much as possible. Plus, you'll be sitting in a classroom, listening to other cars on track, wishing you were out there and not "in this silly waste-of-time-I-know-what-I'm-doing" classroom session. (Note that many "classrooms" at track are less than ideal, including some of which are just a large tent erected in the paddock area.) Add to this that some track classroom instructors aren't always engaging, and you get a situation where you won't learn as much as you should. Later, on the track, your in-car instructor gives you some instructions—important ones, since you're at speed on a track—that you don't understand because that's the part of the classroom session (the part between "Welcome" and "If there are no questions, let's head out to the track") you zoned out on. That can be dangerous.

You don't want to miss the important stuff, so learn all of the driving technique stuff you can at home. Then, what the instructor has to say in the classroom will simply reinforce and clarify the things you've already picked up on

Most at-track high-performance driver education (HPDE) events include a classroom training session.

Learn and prepare as much as you can before going to a track: it will make your time there more productive and fun.

your own. The instructor will cover some extremely important information about how the event will be run, the schedule for the day, rules, and other things that your brain will be too full to soak up if you don't take this approach. Doesn't that sound better? See the Appendix for resources.

I can guarantee that taking a little time and money, investing in learning and preparing before going to the track, will pay off many times over. It may even save you from damaging your car, your body, and, very likely, your ego.

Once you're at the track, use the tools and resources available to you. At first, it'll mostly be your instructor, but over time you can use in-car video, going back to some of the resources you used before coming to the track to clarify your thinking, and maybe various levels of data acquisition.

DATA ACQUISITION SYSTEMS

Some drivers go out and spend hundreds of dollars on a data acquisition system, and then they don't have the bandwidth to use it effectively. In fact, I've talked to drivers who have spent a thousand dollars on a system and haven't looked at it in a year. It's a good joke: there's less expensive ballast if your car is underweight!

Data systems are extremely powerful (and beyond the scope of this book), and I highly recommend using them. But be sure you have the time and ability to make them work for you. Remember that you can buy inexpensive apps that work on a smartphone to give you valuable feedback. Like driving, start slow with your choice of data system and only upgrade it when it's really holding you back.

Also, more and more performance cars have on-board technology that can help you analyze your driving and become a better driver through on-board cameras, recordings of lap times, and data analysis of your performance. Essentially, many cars are equipped from the factory with what was once a data system only available to high-end race teams.

High-performance driving was born on a racetrack, and it takes a level-headed driver to use it responsibly on the road. If applied properly, what you learn driving on a racetrack will make you a better driver on the road. And that depends on your mental skills: what goes on inside your head while driving is the key to high-performance driving.

13 THE MENTAL GAME

What percentage of driving is mental versus physical?

That's a tricky question. If you're like most drivers, though, you'll feel that driving is more of a mental challenge than a physical one. Sure, it takes physical coordination, strength, and stamina to drive at speed on a track (and even on the street); it takes physical skills. No argument there. When you think about it, your body (the physical) doesn't do anything unless your brain commands. You could say that high-performance

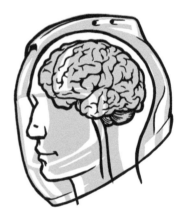

High-performance driving is a demanding mental challenge—it's a mental game.

driving is more mental than physical—perhaps it's even 100 percent mental.

My point is not to find a specific number or answer to this question, but to emphasize just how important the "mental game" is to driving.

As I said in the introduction, you do what you do because you're mentally programmed to do so. Sometimes, you don't do what you want because you either don't have the right programming, or you access the wrong mental program (therefore, making a mistake).

Think about this and understand it. Before you learn a new skill, you don't have the mental programming to do it. That's it, simple as that. As you learn a skill, you build the mental programming, actually developing the neuro-pathways that represent that skill.

Some of the skills you have are programmed to the point where you no longer think about them; you just do them. Some require a little conscious thought, as you're still developing these. And for other skills, you haven't developed neuro-pathways yet, so you have no mental programming to do them.

As I said, every now and then you access the wrong mental program. For example, if you've ever gone to shift from second to third gear in an H-pattern transmission—but instead shifted to fifth—then you know what I'm talking about. You accessed the wrong program, your "shift to fifth" program. Why does that happen? Because you're human.

How do you develop mental programming? Through repetition of the same action, over and over again. Interestingly, that repetition can be physical, or it can be mental. In other words, you can physically repeat the action over and over again, or you can imagine doing that action, over and over again. This is typically called visualization.

I've never met a high-performance driver who spends more time on the track than they do on the street. Even Formula One, Indy car, and NASCAR racers drive more on the road than they do the track. As with them, so with you: every time you drive to work, to the corner store, or to the track, you're physically repeating—and, therefore, programming—your driving skills and techniques. Make the most of this practice.

I was once instructing a high-performance driver on a racetrack, sitting in the passenger seat. As we pulled onto the track from the pit lane, we went through two fairly high-speed left-hand corners, then approached a right-hander. The driver, with two hands on the steering wheel approaching the corner, took his left hand off the wheel and braced his arm on top of the door. Quickly traveling around the track, I noticed that every time the driver turned into a right-hand corner, his left hand came off the steering wheel and he positioned his arm against the door. Why? Because it was a habit, a mental program. How and where had he developed this program? While driving on the road.

Since driving fast through any corner on a track is not as safe or controlled with only one hand working the steering wheel, I told my driver to keep both hands on the wheel. He did. But for many laps this required him to use a small portion of brain power to think about what he was doing with his left arm and hand in right-hand corners.

This is why it's so important to build good habits, good mental programming, while driving on the road. This is why driving on the road can make you a better track driver, and vice versa.

You can also develop practically all of the programming to do any and all techniques and skills I've talked about in this book using mental imagery. You can imagine driving the ideal line around a racetrack; positioning and maneuvering your feet to heel-and-toe downshift; managing your car's weight to control it at or near the limit; positioning your car in the best lane on the street; reading other drivers and the road ahead; being engaged in the act of driving.

The more you imagine high-performance driving, the better a driver you will become. Mental imagery is an incredibly powerful technique, especially if you use more than just your visual sense. If you imagine what you feel, and actually move your body when imagining the skills and techniques you're developing; if you imagine the sounds of the tires, the air rushing past your car, the

SPEED SECRET

Practice doesn't make perfect. Only perfect practice makes perfect.

engine—your mind can't tell the difference between a real and an imagined event. But you need to use at least those three senses for your mind to readily accept the programming. If you only imagine the visual picture, it's not as effective.

To illustrate the power of multisensory mental imagery, imagine a lemon on a table in front of you. It's a bright, shiny, yellow lemon. Imagine picking it up and feeling the shape of the lemon, as well as the texture of the skin. Now, imagine placing that bright yellow lemon on a table in front of you and picking up a knife. You cut through the lemon, hearing the serrated edge of the knife blade cutting the skin of the lemon. As you cut the lemon in half, you notice the lemon juices on the blade of the knife, dripping onto the table. After you've cut the lemon in half, imagine picking up one half in your hand and squeezing it. You feel the juices drip onto your fingers, down your hand. Bring that lemon half up to your nose and smell it. Now squeeze the lemon half again and bring it to your mouth. Lick the juices off the face of the lemon. Taste the lemon.

What just happened? If you're like most people, you puckered up a little, and maybe even some saliva built up in your mouth. Why? Because your mind couldn't tell the difference between a real lemon and one you imagined. If you'd simply imagined the visual image of a lemon, this would likely have not happened. But you used your sight, hearing, touch, smell and taste to imagine the lemon, so your mind thought there was real citric acid coming into your mouth. Your mind triggered saliva to water down the lemon juice.

That's the power of mental imagery, if you use as many senses as possible.

When you imagine driving—the line through corners, the various techniques and skills, and even your mental mindset—use your vision, feel (kinesthetic), and hearing (auditory) senses. The more you see, feel, and hear, the more realistic it is to your mind and the more effective the process of building mental programming will be.

You can develop the skills and techniques you need to be a great high-performance driver by physically doing things, or you can use mental imagery. Which way is the least costly? Which way can you do over and over again without making a mistake, anytime, anywhere?

FOCUS AND DISTRACTIONS

When you're driving on the track, your life depends on your level of concentration. If you lose concentration for even half a second, you could crash. And it's not a stretch to think that driving on the road among drivers with questionable skills and attention is even more dangerous. That's a pretty good motivation to keep your mind on driving! Fortunately, when you're on the track, you have very few distractions. That's not the case when you're driving on the street.

There seem to be more and more distractions around us each day. Not only are there more traffic and street signs to deal with every day: technology is also making attentiveness more difficult. Cell phones, navigation and entertainment systems, and more have become common ingredients in our daily driving.

With our lives becoming busier and busier each day, we try to accomplish more things while driving. Things like shaving, applying makeup, drinking coffee, and eating are becoming common while driving.

But should they be?

When we play golf, we think about golf. When we play the piano, we think about playing the piano. When we're working, we think about work. When we talk to a friend, we think about the conversation. And yet, when we're driving, most drivers think about anything but driving—golf, piano, work, a conversation with a friend . . . .

I'm not saying we all have to drive without looking at, or doing, anything else all of the time. If you're driving in conditions that don't require 100 percent concentration—light traffic, good weather, open road—there's no reason why you can't do a little more than just drive.

In fact, there are benefits with some technology, particularly cell phones. Despite all of the bad press they've gotten, when used properly, cell phones can be beneficial.

With any of these distractions, though, you need to use a little common sense.

On rainy days in rush hour, I've seen drivers talking on cellphones while drinking coffee. Drivers text and send emails while driving on the freeway at 70 miles per hour. I've seen people eating pizza and listening to their stereo at who knows how many decibels.

Who's driving the car? I'm not talking about just the physical action of driving: I'm talking about the mental side of driving. Driving safely in any condition requires far more concentration than most of us care to admit.

If you're going to do something other than drive, use common sense. Pull to the side of the road to make a call; use hands-free technology; wait until a traffic light to reach into the back seat

Most drivers on the street today think about just about anything other than driving: golf, piano, work, a conversation. Practice focusing on the act of driving.

to grab something; pull to the side of the road to load a DVD for the kids; eat in the parking lot of the fast-food outlet; keep your stereo at a reasonable volume so you can concentrate on traffic around you; and shave or apply makeup at home!

If you add up all the time you can save by doing these things while driving, and compare them to the time lost with one minor crash caused by it, you'll be convinced immediately. Concentrate on using common sense. Think about driving.

Since you are human, you're going to lose your focus at times while driving. Even while driving fast

Use a "trigger," such as "Eyes up, look ahead," to help you maintain and regain your mental focus.

around a racetrack it's likely that you'll lose focus. For example, while driving through turn three of a track, you'll think about a mistake you made in turn one. That's not helping you drive turn three any better! And I don't know of a high-performance driver in the world who hasn't had thoughts while driving on the track about where they're going eat dinner that evening. It's almost funny how our minds can drift like that.

Of all the mental challenges that drivers have shared with me, it's maintaining focus that is the most common. But here's the thing: the best race drivers in the world lose their focus just as much as you or anyone else. The difference is the speed at which they regain it, so quickly that it seems as though they never lose it.

When they lose their focus, most drivers think about not losing it. In other words, when they lose focus they tell themselves, "I've lost focus. Come on, focus. Don't think about what happened back there." And in doing so they actually reinforce what they don't want. Drivers who quickly regain focus have a "trigger" for bringing them back into the moment.

You've seen people who have an elastic band on their wrist to help remind them of a habit. Perhaps you've used this technique. The elastic band is a trigger for changing behavior, and you can use something similar when driving. Instead of the elastic band, though, you can use a word or phrase.

For example, if you program using the phrase, "Eyes up—look ahead" every time your mind starts to wander, it'll help bring you back into the act of driving, right now, right here. The more you use this trigger, the better you'll get at regaining your focus. Instead of focusing on what you don't want, it focuses your mind on what you want.

THE "WHAT IF . . ." GAME

The better you understand the theory of controlling a car, the better chance you have of surviving an emergency. You may have never physically had to control a skidding car, but, if you know in your head how to do it, you've got a much better chance of getting out of a potentially dangerous situation.

For example, imagine you're driving along a two-lane highway when you suddenly hit a large puddle of water, causing your car to veer sideways, to aquaplane. If you have no previous knowledge of how to deal with this situation, you'll probably do very little. At best, you will react to what the car is doing, then try to control it.

On the other hand, if you at least know the theory of how to control a car when it aquaplanes, you will be better prepared. Instead of having to wait to see how the car reacts and then responding to that, you will already have a pretty good idea of what the car is going to do and how to deal with it.

Being mentally prepared for an emergency is at least 50 percent of the battle, and you can do this by playing a game I call the "what if . . ." game while driving.

As you drive, try to imagine what would happen if you suddenly hit a large puddle of water, an icy patch, or another car pulled out in front of you. Then, visualize how you would handle the situation.

When one of these situations really do occur, you'll be prepared. No sweat, you can handle it. In fact, you can practice dealing with these situations many times—in your head. And it doesn't matter whether it's real hands-on practice or imagined, it's going to help. Athletes use this type of visualization all the time. You can use it to become a safer driver.

The next time you're driving in city traffic, imagine what you could do if someone ran through a red light in front of you; if someone was tailgating you; if someone changed lanes right next to you, forcing you towards a row of parked cars; and so on.

And when you're on the highway: what could you do if an oncoming passing car was heading directly towards you; if you hit a patch of black ice or heavy snow; if a car suddenly veered in front of you from a freeway entrance ramp.

The "what if . . ." game is another valuable tool that can help make you a safer driver. Plus, while thinking that much about driving, it forces you to be more alert and to concentrate. In today's traffic, that can't be a bad thing. This is performing as a driver at the highest level.

SPEED SECRET

Play the "What if . . ." game to mentally prepare for the unexpected.

14 HIGH-PERFORMANCE DRIVING

High-performance driving—balancing the car's weight and using it to your advantage, using the steering wheel and pedals with finesse, controlling your car at the limit where it's appropriate, carving the ideal line through a corner, squeezing the throttle and having your car squirt out of the corners, controlling this multi-thousand-pound object with the computing power of the space shuttle—it's a magical feeling.

You wouldn't have read this far if you didn't appreciate what I'm talking about. You wouldn't be interested in becoming an even better high-performance driver.

Don't let technology take the joy out of driving. Instead, embrace the technology and work with it. Respect its limitations.

THE PERFECT DRIVER

I'd like you to try a little mental imagery exercise. Top athletes do this in preparation for their sport, and good drivers should, too. Take a moment to think about the "perfect driver." By "perfect driver," I mean what the best driver in the world would be like.

Now, imagine how that perfect driver would drive; in fact, imagine yourself as that perfect driver. See yourself driving. How would you drive? What would you do?

Would you be courteous? See yourself letting a fellow driver slip in the line in front of you, allowing the traffic to flow smoothly. Imagine yourself on the freeway, driving in the right lane, except when passing another vehicle.

How's your concentration level? Are you calm and relaxed? See yourself focused and thinking about your driving, feeling each and every minute movement of the car. Imagine yourself not getting frustrated by other drivers' actions, but rather enjoying the challenge of interacting, even collaborating with them.

How far ahead are you looking down the road, and are you seeing the big picture? See yourself noticing every detail of the things going on around you—to the front, sides, and rear. You check the rearview mirror, notice the vehicles around you with your peripheral vision and the side mirrors. Imagine looking well down the road in front of you, noticing situations almost before they happen.

How's your use of the controls—the steering wheel, gas, brake and clutch pedals, and transmission? Do you use them with a subtle touch—gently and efficiently? Are you driving smoothly? Imagine yourself with two hands on the steering wheel, arcing the wheel into a corner and then smoothly unwinding it. See yourself squeezing down on the gas and brake pedal, then easing up on them. Notice how you gently place the shifter into the next gear with a light touch. Feel yourself totally in control, sensitive to what the car is telling you, capable of reacting confidently to whatever happens.

How do you react to the traffic around you? Are you using your turn signals every time you change lanes or make a turn? See yourself flowing effortlessly through all the traffic, able to predict and react to what other drivers are doing. Notice that other drivers hardly know you're on the road, as you never seem to get in their way.

How would you react in an emergency? A car has pulled out directly in front of you or a child has run into the middle of the street. See yourself calmly and confidently looking for an escape route while quickly squeezing the brakes, releasing your vision and brakes, then steering around the car or child to avoid it.

Now, imagine yourself on a racetrack. How smoothly would you be driving? What would the lines through the corners look, feel, and sound like? Do you feel the tires, do you hear them? What sensory information would you use to tell you that your car is at or near its limit? How would you sense understeer and oversteer? How would you manage your car's handling?

Okay, end of exercise—for now. But now that you've got a good, clear picture of how you would act as the perfect driver, you can begin to be that way in real life. While you're driving, think about all the things you just imagined. Picture yourself doing it, and you can become the perfect driver.

THE PERFECT DRIVE

With this in mind, I'd like to challenge you to play my favorite driving game: "The Perfect Drive."

The Perfect Drive can take place anytime and anywhere—on your way to or from work, a holiday trip, a Sunday drive, to and from the track, at the track, or just going to the corner store. What makes a Perfect Drive is many things, most of which I've mentioned throughout this book.

Personally, I have been trying for years to achieve the Perfect Drive, and even came very, very close late one evening. Yet, even though I've never quite made it, I feel it is one of the most effective tools I use both to increase the enjoyment I receive from driving and to make me safer on the road.

Imagine the concentration and attention required to achieve the Perfect Drive, and you begin to understand how much better a driver you will be while striving for it. Anytime you can make your driving more challenging, the more you will enjoy it—even if you are sitting in rush-hour traffic.

It's hard to define what goes into a Perfect Drive. Just when you think you've covered and perfected everything, the road ahead changes—someone cuts in front of you, the weather changes, the road gets rougher, a corner on a racetrack is off-camber—or your standards for the Perfect Drive rise.

Some of the key aspects that I strive for in *my* Perfect Drive are:

- Proper visual tracking—looking well ahead to where I want the car to be placed
- Planning and thinking well in advance about where I want to go, and the absolute best way to get there
- Making every start (clutch engagement) smooth, with no excessive clutch slippage
- Every shift perfectly smooth—upshifting or downshifting—matching the revs so well that a passenger in the car never feels a single shift
- Returning the clutch foot to the dead pedal immediately after each shift—never riding the clutch pedal
- Turning the steering wheel smoothly, gently, and as little as possible (keeping the front wheels pointing straight as much as possible)—gradually building up cornering forces, then unwinding out of a corner

- Always holding the steering wheel in the 9 and 3 o'clock positions
- Always looking ahead to pick out and predict potential accident situations
- Always driving with an escape route in mind
- Driving the ideal line through every corner
- Braking smoothly and efficiently—and modulating the pedal so that the point where the car actually comes to a complete stop is never felt
- Every lane change made smoothly without running over the reflectors marking the lanes
- Reading road conditions and the other drivers
- Controlling the weight transfer and balance of the car to your advantage
- Before even starting, to ensure the car is prepared to handle a Perfect Drive

Practicing these—and many more—techniques will improve your driving. The increased awareness level necessary to achieve the Perfect Drive will definitely make you a better driver. And, I guarantee, you will enjoy the challenge of everyday driving much more while trying to attain the Perfect Drive.

In closing, I challenge you to attempt your own Perfect Drive. I challenge you to be the best high-performance driver you can be. I challenge you to continue to learn and improve. I challenge you to stay on top of the latest technology in vehicles, adapting to them, and using them for good and not evil.

APPENDIX: SPEED SECRETS

- Use your street driving to make you a better track driver—legally!
- Program the "right" techniques on the street. Practice.
- Focus on learning and continually improving.
- High-performance drivers take full responsibility for their actions, whether "at fault" or not.
- Set an example and drive collaboratively. Others will follow, to everyone's benefit.
- Be honest and accurate with the way you assess the level of risk when driving.
- Help change the world by eliminating the use of the word "accident" to describe car crashes.
- Know what driver and safety aids your vehicle has, how they affect your driving, and what their limitations are.
- Eyes up—look ahead.
- Keep your eyes moving. Scan ahead, to the sides and rear of your vehicle.
- Your hands follow your eyes. Where you look is where you'll steer toward.
- Look where you want to go.
- Drive with a 360-degree view around you.
- Adjust and use your mirrors to ensure you're never surprised by another vehicle.
- High-performance drivers know the importance of the proper seating position.
- Drive with your hands at the 9 and 3 o'clock positions on the steering wheel.
- Turn the steering wheel as little as possible, then straighten it up as soon as you can. Minimize movement of the steering wheel.
- Be aware of the speed at which you turn the steering wheel.
- Initiate slowly, react quickly.
- The less you turn the steering wheel, the faster you will go.
- Be smooth, precise, deliberate, and quick with your use of the pedals.

- Squeeze and ease the throttle—sometimes quickly, always deliberately.
- The initial application and subsequent release of the brakes is what separates the best drivers from the rest.
- The best high-performance drivers can drive any type of transmission.
- Do as little shifting in corners—complete downshifts before, and minimize any upshifts while turning.
- When approaching a corner, use the brakes to slow the car, not the engine by downshifting.
- Heading towards a corner, brake . . . wait . . . then downshift.
- There are no downsides to a smooth downshift!
- Shift—blip—release clutch.
- Practice heel-and-toe downshifting until it becomes something you can do without thinking—a habit.
- The less you do with the controls, the fewer errors you'll make, and the smoother and faster you'll drive.
- The better your understanding of your tires, the better a high-performance driver you'll be.
- The further ahead you look, the smoother you'll drive.
- Smooth is fast.
- As a high-performance driver, you're a weight manager.
- Control understeer and oversteer with your vision and by managing weight transfer.
- The more references you have and use, the better a driver you'll be.
- The larger the radius you drive, the faster you'll go through that specific corner.
- Use corners to maximize your straightaway speed.
- Drive the ideal line to maximize your exit out of the corner and subsequent straightaway speed.
- High-performance driving is a series of compromises.
- The slower the corner, the later the apex, and the quicker and crisper you need to turn the steering wheel—and vice versa.
- Focus on learning to drive the fastest corners first.
- Carry entry speed by looking into the turn and focusing on your release of the brakes. Focus on the end-of-braking (EoB) point.
- You can only ever get 100 percent out of your tires, but that can be used for a combination of traction forces.

- How and when you release the brakes will have more effect on how quickly you can drive than where you start braking.
- In tight, slow corners, use trail braking to help rotate the car; in fast, sweeping corners, reduce the amount you trail brake.
- Adapt your brake release and turning of the steering wheel to the shape of the corner.
- Use a hard initial application of the brakes and gradually bleed off the pressure.
- Read the road.
- Read other drivers.
- Drive collaboratively.
- Drive at an appropriate speed to match the risk level at that very moment.
- Be aware of the speed at which you drive.
- Get and use the best safety equipment possible.
- Learn to drive a slow car fast so you don't end up driving a fast car slow.
- When you can consistently recognize when the driver aids are assisting you—or even saving your butt from crashing—then, and only then, should you consider turning them off.
- You'll always get more improvement out of your own driving than you will out of your car.
- Learn and prepare as much as you can before going to a track: it will make your time there more productive and fun.
- Practice doesn't make perfect. Only perfect practice makes perfect.
- Use mental imagery to build the programming in your mind.
- Regain your focus with a trigger phrase.
- Play the "what if . . ." game to mentally prepare for the unexpected.

RESOURCES

Speed Secrets (speedsecrets.com)—The site for all of my products and services, from free eBooks to webinars and seminars, free driving tips to one-on-one coaching

Learn.SpeedSecrets.com (learn.speedsecrets.com)—My site for access to eCourses to help you prepare before you go to a track

Audi Club North America (www.audiclubna.org)

BMW Car Club of America (www.bmwcca.org)

Porsche Club of America (www.pca.org)

Lockton Affinity Motorsport (locktonmotorsports.com)—Coverage for your car while driving on a racetrack

MotorsportReg (www.motorsportreg.com)—The largest site for registration into all sorts of driving events

Hooked on Driving (www.hookedondriving.com)—A for-profit HPDE event organizer with a strong culture around instruction

Motorsport Safety Foundation (www.motorsport-safety.org)—A nonprofit organization dedicated to making all forms of motorsports safer

INDEX

ABOUT THE AUTHOR

Ross Bentley has been training drivers since 1980. In that time, he's taught teens the basics of driving, Navy SEALs and elite police forces advanced driving techniques, and average motorists how to survive on their daily commute. He's coached race drivers of every level, from beginners to elite-level professionals in everything from NASCAR to Indy cars, prototype sports cars to go karts, rally and rallycross to drag racers, and even motorcycle racers. Ross is especially passionate about educating and training high-performance drivers who participate in HPDE and track day events for the pure love of it.

Ross's experience behind the wheel inspired his love for helping other drivers improve, having raced mostly in open-wheel (Indy car, Formula Atlantic, Formula Ford) and sports cars (prototypes, GT, Trans-Am). He won the 1998 United States Road Racing Championship driving for the factory BMW team, as well as the 2003 Rolex 24-Hours of Daytona. When the opportunity presents itself, Ross continues to race.

This is Ross's eighth Speed Secrets book. He writes articles for a variety of online and print media, as well as sharing tips on his website and through social media.

Ross's Speed Secrets Driver Development products and services include:

- eCourses
- e-Newsletter
- eBooks
- One-on-one coaching
- Remote coaching
- Seminars and workshops for groups
- Webinars

For more information about these products and services, please visit www.speedsecrets.com.